American Crossroads

American Crossroads

The Intersection of Christianity and Democracy

Jesse Wisnewski

RESOURCE *Publications* • Eugene, Oregon

AMERICAN CROSSROADS
The Intersection of Christianity and Democracy

Resource Publications
An Imprint of Wipf and Stock Publishers
199 W. 8th Ave., Suite 3
Eugene, OR 97401

www.wipfandstock.com

ISBN 13: 978-1-61097-607-7

Manufactured in the U.S.A.

This book is dedicated to my wife and children. Your presence and love makes an immeasurable difference in my life.

"Of all the dispositions and habits which lead to political prosperity, religion and morality are indispensable supports. In vain would that man claim the tribute of patriotism, who should labor to subvert these great pillars of human happiness, these firmest props of the duties of men and citizens. The mere politician, equally with the pious man, ought to respect and to cherish them. A volume could not trace all their connections with private and public felicity. Let it simply be asked: Where is the security for property, for reputation, for life, if the sense of religious obligation desert the oaths which are the instruments of investigation in courts of justice? And let us with caution indulge the supposition that morality can be maintained without religion. Whatever may be conceded to the influence of refined education on minds of peculiar structure, reason and experience both forbid us to expect that national morality can prevail in exclusion of religious principle."

—George Washington's Farewell Address

Contents

Introduction

Fulfilling the Call

WHAT FOLLOWS is not an endorsement or slander of any president, political party, public policy, or political theory.[1] It is not an extensive treatment of political theory or a historical treatise on the relationship between the church and state. What follows is much simpler than this.

What follows is best described as a call, a call to Christians, a call to stand up and fulfill our societal obligations by influencing the Democratic process of the United States of America distinctly as believers and followers of Jesus Christ.

This is a call to those are who are currently disengaged or disenfranchised with the political process. It is also a call to those who were once politically involved to consider getting involved once again.

And finally, this is a call to those who are currently engaged in the political realm. Regardless of whether you are a conscientious voter, lobbyist, pastor, or legislator, this is a call for you to consider whether or not your

1. With this work I cite a range of sources, drawing from such Christian traditions as Reformed, Lutheran, Baptist, and Anabaptist. These different streams of thought will at times lead their adherents to differing positions on public policy and political theory. With this being said, the citation of an author's work is not an endorsement of their theological persuasions or public policy opinions.

involvement is truly God-honoring, Christ-exalting, and Spirit-empowered.

In writing this piece I primarily worked from Romans 13.1–7, unfolding what it means for Christians to be submissive to the government within our distinct American context. My goal is that we will come away with a clearer understanding of what it means to be submissive to the government of the United States of America as believers and followers of Jesus Christ. In addition, it is my desire to address common rebuttals from both Christians and non-Christians alike who contend for the exclusion of Christians in particular and faith in general from the political process.

PUTTING THINGS IN PERSPECTIVE

This is not the first time in the history of Christianity that the fog needs to be cleared in order for us to see what exactly our relationship with the government should be. John Stott rightly observed that "relations between church and state have been notoriously controversial throughout the Christian centuries."[2] It is this issue that needed to be addressed in ancient Rome, and the Apostle Paul did so in his letter to the Christians there. To help us understand the significance of Paul's words in Romans 13.1–7, it is imperative

2. Stott, *The Message of Roman*, 339. John Stott provided the following simplification of church state models: "Erastianism (the state controls the church), theocracy (the church controls the state), Constantinianism (the compromise in which the state favors the church and the church accommodates to the state in order to retain its favor), and partnership (church and state recognize and encourage each other's distinct God-given responsibilities in a spirit of constructive collaboration). The fourth seems to accord best with Paul's teaching in Romans 13" (339).

for us to observe its greater context, namely Romans 12 and 13.11–14.

HEAVENLY CITIZENS

In Romans 12.2 Paul asserts that Christians are not to be conformed to "this world," which means "this age."[3] In other words, we are to "resist the pressure of being squeezed into the mold of this world and the pattern of behavior that typifies it."[4] This is why it is of extreme importance that we are made aware of what is and is not influencing and determining our worldview - the overall way that we see and interpret things - especially in relationship to our political opinions.

Instead of being conformed in this way, Paul declares that Christians are to "be transformed by the renewal of your mind, that by testing you may discern what is the will of God, what is good and acceptable and perfect" (Rom 12.2).[5]

We must understand that as Christians we are not only citizens of America, but we are primarily citizens of heaven through our faith in Jesus Christ, which supersedes our responsibilities to Caesar (Phil 3.20; cf.1.27–30). It is for this reason that God calls us to "Set your minds on things that are above, not on things that are on earth. For

3. Moo, *The Epistle to the Romans*, 755. From the footnotes of Moo's commentary, we read that the "Greek *aiōn* can refer to the 'word' in a spatial sense but typically in Paul it has a temporal nuance, referring to 'this age' as the period of time in world history characterized by the domination of sin and Satan."

4 Ibid., 755.

5. Unless otherwise indicated, the *English Standard Version* translation will be used throughout this book.

you have died, and your life is hidden with Christ in God" (Col 3.2–3).

As Christians, our primary allegiance is not to any governor, state, president, policy, or political party, but to the Lord of lords and King of kings, Jesus Christ. We must bear this reality in mind as we read Romans.

THE RETURN OF JESUS CHRIST

In Romans 13.11–14 Paul is pointing his audience to the unquestionable return of the Lord Jesus Christ, which indicates the consummation—the ultimate end, fulfillment, and perfection—of all things.[6]

Now, if we keep in mind the first thought from Romans 12.1–2 (our main citizenry is in heaven) and the second one from Romans 13.11–14 (Jesus will return), we can see why Paul may have included his call for Christians to submit to the governing authorities in Romans 13.1–7.[7]

TYING IT ALL TOGETHER

In order for Paul to safeguard against people drawing the wrong conclusions about his teachings, he may have included these thoughts as a precursor to combating extremism (i.e. the casting off of societal responsibilities).[8] In his commentary on the Book of Romans, Douglas Moo said:

> Paul's teaching about the transitory nature of this world might be precisely why he includes 13.1–7.

6. Morris, *The Epistle to the Romans*, 470–71.
7. Moo, 791.
8. Mott, *Biblical Ethics and Social Change*, 148.

> His purpose may be to stifle the kind of extremism that would pervert his emphasis on the coming of a new era and on the 'new creation' into a rejection of every human and society convention—including the government.[9]

Dr. Moo went on to say that "'Not being conformed to this world' does not require Christians to renounce every institution now in place in society. After all, some institutions, such as government and marriage, reflect God's providential ordering of the world for our good and His glory."[10] For us today, this simply means that Christians do not have an obligation to renounce the government or any other societal institution like family, education, art, and business.

With the existence of this rebellious tendency amongst the people, we can reason that Paul emphasized the subjection of Christians to the governing authorities as a means of fulfilling God's revealed will for their lives (hence Rom 12.2).

As we look to be faithful to the call of God upon our lives by submitting to the government of the United States, it is essential for us to know what this looks like and how we should do so within our distinct American context. This is why it is imperative for us to understand what Paul meant by his discussion of submission in Romans 13.1.

9. Moo, 791. Knowing that Paul has been considered the apostle of Christian freedom (Bennett, *Christians and the State*, 132), it is easy to see that particularly within the Pauline churches "there were Christians who overemphasized and misused their freedom in connection with their spiritual gifts . . . As a result; they sought to cast off the duties of their roles in society . . ." (Mott, 148).

10. Ibid., 803.

1

Submitting to the Government

What it Means and Why it's Important

THE APOSTLE Paul wrote the Book of Romans sometime between the years of A.D. 54 and A.D. 59.[1] It is in this letter, particularly in the 13th chapter, that he addresses the issue of his recipient's relationship with the existing Roman government.

Paul wrote in Romans 13.1: "Let every person be *subject* to the governing authorities. (Italics mine). It has been said that this command defines the most rudimentary aspect of the relationship between Christians and the state. If this foundational concept of submission is not rightly understood, then our relationship as Christians to the state will rest upon faulty ground. Besides, this passage has been misapplied in the past, causing incalculable suffering in the world.[2]

As Christians, our understanding of submission to the state is very important and will affect the way that we relate to the government of the United States of America.

1. Ibid., 3.

2. Cullman, *The State in the New Testament*, 55, taken from Stott, 341.

The concept of obedience is inherent to submission, along with its correlative warnings of rebellion against the state.[3] Moreover, in the remainder of this passage—Rom 13.1–7—we observe that every Christian is told to be in subjection to the governing authorities for there is no authority except from God, all authority is established by God, and that governing rulers are considered servants of God (Rom 13.2, 6). This is why John Stott strongly cautioned: "For this reason they [submission, rebellion, and obedience] have constantly been misapplied by oppressive right-wing regimes, as if Scripture gave rulers carte blanche to develop a tyranny and to demand unconditional obedience."[4]

What do we make of submission? How are we to submit? Are we to understand this passage as calling for unquestionable obedience to the governing authorities, whether they are of the United States of America, Canada, Australia, China, Venezuela, or Iran? Without using fancy verbal gymnastics, how can we understand this commandment of God as anything else other than absolute?

WHAT DOES SUBMISSION MEAN?

In Romans 13.1, the Greek work that is translated as "submission" in English is the Greek word *hypotasso*. This is a complex word and can denote either an enforced or voluntary submission.[5] This Greek word finds its root in the

3. Stott, 341.

4. Ibid.

5. Neufeld, "Submission to Governing Authorities: A Study of Romans 13.1–7," 93; and, Bauer, *A Greek English Lexicon of the New Testament and Other Early Christian Literature*, 848.

combination of the Greek preposition *hypo* with the verb *tasso*. The general meaning of *hypo* is "under" or "below" and the basic meaning of *tasso* is "to appoint, to order, to arrange, to determine, to set in place, [and] to establish."[6] It is the combination of these two words that forms *hypotasso*.

Now that we have a basic understanding of what this word means, let us consider a couple of examples of how this word is used elsewhere in the New Testament.

In Luke 10.1 we read that Jesus Christ appointed and sent out seventy people in pairs ahead of Him to every city and place to which He was going. After their departure, we read of their joyful return in Luke 10.17, in which they boast, "Lord, even the demons are subject (*hypotasso*) to us in your name." What we see in this one instance is that demons were forced to submit to the seventy in the name of Jesus Christ. This use of the word *hypotasso* observably implies a forced submission or subjection.

In James 4.7 we read, "Submit (*hypotasso*) yourselves therefore to God." In this passage we see that the Greek word for submit is used in a voluntary sense. James calls upon us to submit voluntarily to God.

If *hypotasso* can mean either a forced or voluntary submission, we must answer this all-important question,

> "Are we to submit to the governing authorities as the demons were to the name of Jesus, or are we to submit to the government in the way that James calls us to submit to God?"

6. Kittel and Friedrich, *Theological Dictionary of the New Testament*, 1156.

Based upon the context of this passage (Rom 13.1–7), I believe that the Greek word *hypotasso* takes on a voluntary meaning similar to that of James. Let me explain.

When we attempt to determine the meaning of a word in any given context, we must first determine the word's range of meaning, just like we did above. Afterwards, we must determine how it is used in the specific passage, which is only possible by understanding how its meaning is influenced by the immediate context, section, book, author, testament, Bible, and genre.[7]

In Romans 13.1, *hypotasso* is used in the present-middle-imperative-third-person-singular form. What this means for us is that this word, as used by Paul in Romans 13.1, indicates a continuous action[8] and suggestive element.[9] In teasing out the meaning of this word, to submit in this passage means "to subject oneself, to be subservient, to submit voluntarily."[10] We see this meaning further supported in other sections of this passage, namely Rom 12.9–21 and 13.8–14.

In these sections Paul emphasizes acts of selfless love.[11] Due to Romans 13.1–7 being linked with the preceding and following passages,[12] we can reason that Paul's emphasis on

7. Osborne, *The Hermeneutical Spiral*, 22.

8. Mounce, *Basics of Biblical Greek*, 311.

9. This latter observation is based upon the transitive nature of the verbs that can be utilized in order to make sense of the construction (Mounce, 311).

10. Bromiley, 1157; Moo, 797 and 809.

11. Neufeld, 93; Yoder, *The Politics of Jesus*, 196.

12. Yoder added that "[Romans] 13.8 begins with a verbal echo of verse 7. . .[and] the submission to the powers in 13.1 is motivated and exposited by the hope in 13.11–14. Verse 10, by expositing verse

selfless love allows us to press a voluntary meaning of submission from Romans 13.1.

What is more, Paul called for everyone to "submit" rather than to "obey" the governing authorities.[13] This fine distinction of words enables us to understand that Paul was calling his recipients to subject themselves voluntarily to the Roman government.[14]

Based upon the tense of *hypotasso* the context of Romans 12–13, and Paul's call for "submission" rather than "obedience," it can be deduced that Paul implied a voluntary and reflective submission to the governing authorities rather than an enforced submission. This has some very practical application for us today.

First of all, I hope you see that to be submitted to the government does not require us to give up independent thought, nor does it insinuate that we are somehow unequal and inferior to the institution of government. This is not the case at all. Being voluntarily submitted to the government refers to our posture towards government, not our inferiority.

Secondly, given that every government is ordained by God, Christians are to acknowledge this status and recognize that government has a God-given right to demand our allegiance. It is for this reason that we must generally obey what the government asks of us, but not in every particular

---

8, also gives a definition of the 'good' in verse 3, whereby the behavior of Christians under government is guided."

13. Moo, 797; Yoder, 209.

14. Ibid., 797. "One's submission to government is to be superseded by their submission to God. For "all subordinate 'submissions' must always be measured in relationship to our all-embracing submission to God" (Moo, 797).

case. After all, the government does not possess an absolute power over our lives—especially here in America—because the government's authority is delegated and limited by God (more on this later).

"This means," begins Douglas Moo, "that Christians may continue to 'submit' to a particular government even as they, in obedience to a 'higher' authority, refuse to do, in a given instance, what the government requires." Dr. Moo also goes on to explain how this works out in marriage. "In a similar way, the Christian wife, called on to 'submit' to her husband, may well have to disobey a particular request of her husband if it conflicts with her allegiance to God."[15]

Since Paul wrote this letter to the Christians in Rome, who lived under the rule of a government that was much different than ours today, how are we to apply it to our modern lives? This is the topic that will be explored next.

15. Ibid., 809.

2

A Call to Influence the Government

Submitting to the Government of the United States is a Call to Influence the Government of the United States

DURING THE TIME that Paul wrote this letter to the Christians in Rome, the Roman government was not built upon the will of the people. Like many governments in the world today, it was not established to promote justice or the welfare of the people, but rather to support and further the interests of the leaders in Rome.[1] The concept of government as an extension of the people would have been unimaginable to Paul.[2]

If we were to conduct a general overview of ancient history we would discover that governments usually were some form of hierarchy that often enforced its will upon the people through military might and oppression. In fact, it wouldn't be long after Paul wrote this letter that the Roman

1. Jeffers, *The Greco-Roman World of the New Testament*, 110.

2. Isaak, "The Christian Community and Political Responsibility," 37.

government, under the leadership of Nero, would ruthlessly persecute Christians, claiming the lives of Paul and Peter.[3]

For someone to be in subjection to the governing authorities of Rome in the 1st century would look entirely different from someone being in submission to the governing authorities of the United States of America in the 21st century. Our government is completely different from ancient Rome's; our government is dependent upon the involvement of each and every single one of its citizens for its wellbeing as well as ours.

Our current form of government took shape through the minds and pens of our early founding fathers, as can be seen in the first two paragraphs of the Declaration of Independence:

> When in the Course of human events, it becomes necessary for one people to dissolve the political bands which have connected them with another, and to assume among the powers of the earth, the separate and equal station to which the Laws of Nature and of Nature's God entitle them, a decent respect to the opinions of mankind requires that they should declare the causes which impel them to the separation.
>
> We hold these truths to be self-evident, that all men are created equal, that they are endowed by their Creator with certain unalienable Rights, that among these are Life, Liberty, and the pursuit of happiness—That to secure these rights, Governments are instituted among Men,

3. Gundry, *A Survey of the New Testament*, 12.

> deriving their just powers from the consent of the governed.

Clearly the authors and signers of this document believed in the self-evident proof of nature that proceeds from an external and transcendent God, and that governments are established by those they serve and derive their powers from the people they govern.

Thus, government officials such as presidents, members of congress, state governors, and town mayors are not to govern apart from the authority the United States Constitution, or the will of the people they serve. These officials do not obtain their position through individual effort alone. These officials obtain their position by the votes of people whom they are to represent in their respective area of governmental responsibility.

Our government was founded by the people and for the people, and derives its powers not from those in office, but from those whom it serves. This is why Tom Minnery, author of Why You Can't Stay Silent, said:

> Unlike the Roman Empire in the first century, our country is a participatory republic. We have the obligation to make our views heard and to get involved in dialogue. Our government asks us, as citizens, to participate, not merely to shut up and obey. "We the people" means Christians as well as non-Christians. Submission in our political system includes being willing to contribute to the political process, not withdraw from it.[4]

4. Minnery, *Why You Can't Stat Silent*, 100.

As American citizens we possess an awesome and historically unique privilege and responsibility to be involved within the political process.[5]

THE LIMITATION OF GOVERNMENT POWER

With the Declaration of Independence as the foundation, the role of the governed was further built upon in the Constitution of the United States of America. From the preamble of our Constitution, we read:

> We the People of the United States, in order to form a more perfect Union, establish Justice, insure domestic Tranquility, provide for the common defense, promote the general Welfare, and secure the Blessings of Liberty to ourselves and our Posterity, do ordain and establish this Constitution of the United States of America.

What we observe here is an intended delegation of limited powers to the governing authorities. "The people delegate certain powers to government; government has no powers other than those delegated," remarked John Eidsmoe.[6] Consequently, elected representatives in our country are to serve the people who voted them in under the authority of the Constitution. Governing apart from these limitations will inevitably lead to tyranny at the hands of a few, not the many.[7] By stating in an unchanging Constitution[8] what the

5. Colson, *Kingdoms in Conflict*, 278.

6. Eidsmoe, *Christianity and the Constitution*, 372.

7. Noebel, *Understanding the Time*, 299.

8. Although some may disagree, I see that the United States of America's Constitution has an unchanging meaning and application

government can and cannot do, our early founders created "a form of government that, while based on popular consent and some popular participation, places obstacles in the path of majoritarian democracy and limits the purposes and powers of the government in order to prevent tyranny."[9]

THE WELL-BEING OF OUR GOVERNMENT IS DEPENDENT UPON THE PEOPLE IT SERVES

Our government cannot exist without the participation of American citizens or our obedience to its laws. If we neglect our role and responsibility, then we run the risk of allowing our government to develop into a totalitarian regime without opposition. It is said that "widespread participation in politics—including voting in elections, contacting public officials, working with others to bring matters to public attention, joining associations that work to shape government actions, and more—is necessary to ensure not only that responsive representatives will be chosen, but that they will have continuous incentives to pay attention to the people. Because widespread participation is so central to popular sovereignty, we can say that the less political participation there is in a society, the weaker the democracy."[10]

Those who shy away from and even scorn our political process are committing an injustice against themselves

---

for the following two reasons. First, the early founders believed that its intended meaning was to continue (Barton, *Original Intent*). Second, since it was written with an intended purpose that is now rooted in history, the meaning of this document carries with it an unchanging meaning.

9. Ibid., 373.

10. Greenberg and Page, *The Struggle for Democracy*, 9.

and their neighbors. Besides, those who contend for a non-participatory position are by default promoting a form of involvement.[11]

Even though this is the case, there are some lingering questions that remain. How does this apply to Christians? Are we obligated to influence the political processes of America? How can we reconcile involvement in worldly government with such Christian principals as not being "conformed to this world," (Rom 12.2) and to be in the world, but not a part of it (John 17.11, 14–15)? Besides, aren't politics dirty and sinful, automatically demanding compromise of Christian principles and convictions?

OUR SUBMISSION IS TO THE EXISTING FORM OF GOVERNMENT

Just as God through Paul was calling for Christians to submit to the Roman government that forced its will upon the people, so too is God through Paul calling for us to submit to our form of government in America (Rom 13.1), a government that lives and thrives on the will and involvement of the people.

As American citizens we have an obligation to promote the justice and welfare of all people, both born and unborn. Unlike many in history and the world today, we have a right to the freedom of speech and assembly, and we have a legitimate duty to praise and criticize public officials and government policies "by calling government to fulfill its proper task and high purpose" of promoting justice and

11. Kyle, "Anabaptist and Reformed Attitudes Towards Civil Government."

the welfare of the people.[12] Without the active involvement of every American citizen, our government cannot exist and would inevitably morph into a totalitarian regime governed by the few and not the representatives of the many.

SUBMITTING TO THE GOVERNMENT NECESSITATES OUR INVOLVEMENT

For Christians to be submitted to the government is the same as "placing ourselves under" its authority, acknowledging its role and purpose in our lives as established by God.[13] Since our government depends upon our involvement and we are called to submit ourselves to the governing authorities, then we—as Christians—are willed by God to influence the political process (Rom 12.2). Just as God called for everyone to submit to the Roman government that forced its will upon the people, so too is God calling for everyone to submit to our form of government in the United States of America, a government that is dependent upon the involvement of the people.

During the time that Paul was writing his letter, to associate freely and speak against the government was discouraged and punished, just like it would be today in communist countries like China and Cuba, or authoritarian regimes like Sudan, Vietnam, and North Korea.

It's easy to take for granted the freedoms that we so readily enjoy in America. If we currently lived in an

12. "Guidelines for Government and Citizenship, " The Center for Public Justice, accessed December 10, 2011, http://www.cpjustice.org/content/government.

13. Isaak, 41; Moo, 798.

authoritarian regime, we would have no guarantee of civil liberties, such as the freedom of speech and assembly. Authoritarian governments are known to suppress and disperse competitors and challengers through a highly centralized government that maintains political stability and security through military might. The citizen of such a country who speaks against the policies of his or her government will do so with the expectation of being penalized, imprisoned, tortured, or killed. For a person to be in submission to the governing authorities of such countries is entirely different than it is here in America.

The well-being and survival of our government depends upon the involvement of its citizens. For us to be in submission to our form of government here in America necessitates that we—as Christian citizens—are involved within the political process. In the words of Charles Colson, "as citizens of the nation-state, Christians have the same civic duties all citizens have: to serve on juries, to pay taxes, to vote, to support candidates they think are best qualified."[14]

Our involvement within the political process demands that we strike a balance. For instance, our submission to the government necessitates that our involvement within the democratic process is to be done distinctly as Christians. This means that our faith is not to be separated from our political thoughts, words, and actions. Our faith is to serve as the foundation and guiding force in our political positions and involvement.

Our responsibilities as citizens to our great republic are not fulfilled by simply voting. Christian citizens have an obligation to participate in the process just as

14. Colson, 278.

non-Christians do, which includes voting, contacting public officials, working with others to bring matters to public attention, campaigning, joining associations that work to shape government actions, and even becoming government leaders.

This flies in the face of the oft-invoked argument that we are to be concerned only with living and sharing the Gospel of Jesus Christ and not entangled with the affairs of this world, especially the political process.

SHOULD CHRISTIANS PRIMARILY BE CONCERNED WITH EVANGELISM, NOT POLITICAL AFFAIRS?

Even though he does not call for the complete avoidance of political or civic causes, John MacArthur—whom I greatly respect and admire—does bring attention to the temporal benefit of our submission to the government in his book *Why the Government Can't Save You*. In his opinion, it is appropriate for Christians to be involved within the political process when we realize "that such interest is not vital to our spiritual growth, our righteous testimony, or the advancement of the kingdom of Christ."[15]

MacArthur further claims that "God does not call the church to influence the culture by promoting legislation and court rulings that advance a scriptural point of view. Nor does He condone any type of radical activism that would avoid tax obligations, disobey or seek removal of government officials we don't agree with, or spend an inordinate

15. MacArthur, *Why Government Can't Save You*, 8.

amount of time campaigning for a so-called Christian slate of candidates."

In the end, Dr. MacArthur's argument is not entirely without merit, but it is not comprehensive and final. Let me explain.

If our involvement in the political process—or any part of the world for that matter—is at the expense of our relationship with Jesus Christ then we should not be involved. In other words, if our involvement in anything, such as business, law, arts, entertainment, or government, requires us to denounce God in our beliefs and actions then we are to renounce these obligations and turn to God. Our relationship with God through Christ comes first. However, I disagree that Christians are to be concerned solely with living and sharing the Gospel and not worldly affairs in general, and governmental affairs in particular. Ultimately, I think this is too narrow a definition of the Gospel.

THE GOSPEL IS MORE THAN "WINNING" SOULS

It has been said by John MacArthur, and I presume countless others, that "God has above all else called the church to bring sinful people to salvation through Jesus Christ."[16] He goes on to say, "If we do not evangelize the lost and make disciples of new converts, nothing else we do for people—no matter how beneficial it seems—is of any eternal consequence."

To say that anything else we do is of no eternal consequence is to imply that it would be appropriate to overlook the temporal needs of others as if they are of no concern

16. Ibid., 13.

to God. Is this really the case? Does God only care about evangelism? I don't think so. In fact, Jesus had some strong words for those who neglected the needs of others.

At the Final Judgment, we have an image of God sitting upon a throne with the entirety of all the nations gathered before Him. During this time He will separate everyone into two different groups (Matt 25.31–33). One group will inherit "eternal life" and the other group "will go away into eternal punishment" (Matt 25.34, 46). Do you know what the distinguishing factor is between these two groups? It is faith in Jesus Christ that is expressed in good works. We see this in the words of Jesus, who said:

> . . . For I was hungry and you gave me food, I was thirsty and you gave me drink, I was a stranger and you welcomed me, I was naked and you clothed me, I was sick and you visited me, I was in prison and you came to me.' Then the righteous will answer him, saying, 'Lord, when did we see you hungry and feed you, or thirsty and give you drink? And when did we see you a stranger and welcome you, or naked and clothe you? And when did we see you sick or in prison and visit you?' And the King will answer them, 'Truly, I say to you, as you did it to one of the least of these my brothers, you did it to me.' (Matt 25.35–40).

Jesus taught that we are not only responsible for evangelism, but for expressing our faith in Him by loving others (cf. Matt 7.21–23). We see that a similar thought is picked up elsewhere in the New Testament.

We read in the Letter of James, "What good is it, my brothers, if someone says he has faith but does not have works? Can that faith save him? If a brother or sister is poorly clothed and lacking in daily food, and one of you says to them, "Go in peace, be warmed and filled," without giving them the things needed for the body, what good is that? So also faith by itself, if it does not have works, is dead" (Jas 2.14–17).

Moreover, this is recapitulated by the Apostle John, who said, "But if anyone has the world's goods and sees his brother in need, yet closes his heart against him, how does God's love abide in him? Little children, let us not love in word or talk but in deed and in truth" (1 John 3.17–18).

Even though we are justified before God through faith alone in the life, death, and resurrection of Jesus Christ (Rom 3.21–25; 4.1–5; Gal 2.16; Eph 2.1–10), true faith is never alone.[17] In other words, true faith in Jesus Christ will lead a person to do good works, which serve as a means of validating that our faith is real (Rom 6.10; 8.29–30; 2 Cor 5.17; Phil 2.12–13; 1 Pet 1.5–11).

In light of what we just read, I question how MacArthur and others can adhere to their position with such certainty.

We can and must give needy people the Gospel, for it is the power of God unto salvation (Rom 1.17). We are to disciple new converts, teaching them to observe all that Jesus has commanded (Matt 28.16–20). But our responsibilities

17. With this there are two opposing extremes. First, to say that we are justified by God through faith in Jesus Christ plus good works, or by good works alone, is to embrace legalism. Second, to say that we are justified by a faith that reveals no corresponding behavior, then we are embracing another error: anitnominaism (Sproul, *Essential Truths of the Christian Faith*, 191).

do not stop there. We are to minister to the entire person, soul and body, without preferring one over the other. More to the point, if we adhered strictly to MacArthur's position, would this mean that we shouldn't provide for the basic needs of impoverished people who are not Christians?

Even though God has called His people to evangelize, He did not call us to stop there in our responsibilities. God's commandment to go and make disciples of all nations (Matt 28.18–20) does not supersede nor precede our love for God and others that is to be expressed with all of our heart, soul, mind, and strength (Matt 22.34–40).

The Gospel demands our full-orbed obedience to all that the Lord commands. Instead of giving our personal preference to some of God's commandments over others, we must strive in the power of His Spirit to submit the entirety of our lives to the whole counsel and authority of God. This is why preference should not to be given to evangelism or social responsibility alone. These actions should be fused into a whole and not compartmentalized as if they are competing activities. We are called to evangelize and to do good to others (Matt 5.16; Gal 6.10; Eph 4.28; 1 Tim 6.18; 1 Thess 5.15). Evangelism and social responsibility are "like the two blades of a pair of scissors or the two wings of a bird."[18]

May we humbly heed the words of James Daane, who said in response to those who deemed certain actions to be of less priority than others:

> Those who claim that "the primary task of the church is to preach the Gospel" do not really

18. Minnery, 49.

> believe that the church has either spare time or a secondary task. Instead of classifying the tasks that God gives to us as primary and secondary, we should respond with the humility of wholehearted obedience. "We are unprofitable servants. What we ought to do we have done" (Luke 17.10).[19]

The Gospel and social responsibility can and do exist side-by-side without conflict or subordination.[20] Though not adding to or taking away from our right standing with God, good works are a natural result of a life transformed through faith in Christ and will lead people to give glory to God, not deride Him (Matt 5.13–16).

POLITICAL INVOLVEMENT DOES NOT IMPEDE EVANGELISTIC EFFORTS

At this point, some will understandably contend that a person's distinct Christian witness in the public square could impede evangelistic efforts because his or her message will offend others to the point that they will be repulsed by the Gospel. Consider the following example for a point of illustration.

During the height of the Civil Rights Movement, "Jimmy Allen was chided for a strong statement against racial injustice: 'When you as a Baptist preacher get into that kind of controversy, you cut off my chance as a Baptist to win my neighbor who has racial prejudice.'" In response to this rebuke, Mr. Allen pithily responded, "Evangelism

19. Mott, 127.

20. Ibid., 125.

is not tricking people into signing the policy and then letting them read the small print."[21] In a more contemporary vein of thought, we may hear similar reasoning from those who rebuke their brothers and sisters in Christ for speaking out against controversial topics like same-sex marriage, abortion, and religious freedom. Many will express similar concern as our Baptist friend in the example above.

As Christians we cannot balk at proclaiming injustices within social and political spheres. If the governing authorities are committing injustices then we are obligated to speak out against them, bringing these injustices more in line with God's original intent and standards.

A theme of alleviating the oppressed and fighting against injustice is woven throughout the Old and New Testament. Consider just the following example:

> Thus says the LORD: Do justice and righteousness, and deliver from the hand of the oppressor him who has been robbed. And do no wrong or violence to the resident alien, the fatherless, and the widow, nor shed innocent blood in this place (Jer 22.3).

> Wash yourselves; make yourselves clean; remove the evil of your deeds from before my eyes; cease to do evil, learn to do good; seek justice, correct oppression; bring justice to the fatherless, plead the widow's cause (Isa 1.16–17)

> He has told you, O man, what is good; and what does the LORD require of you but to do justice, and to love kindness, and to walk humbly with your God? (Mic 6.8).

21. Mott, 125.

> And the King will answer them, "Truly, I say to you, as you did it to one of the least of these my brothers, you did it to me" (Matt 25.40).

> Religion that is pure and undefiled before God, the Father, is this: to visit orphans and widows in their affliction, and to keep oneself unstained from the world (Jas 1.27).

Evangelism and social responsibility are not two distinct options. It's not one or the other. Evangelism and social responsibility are both foundational to living a life fully committed to the Kingdom of God on earth, as it is in heaven.

The Gospel is more than a message of individual salvation; it is a message about the Kingdom of God (Mark 1.15), which "means nothing less than the reign of God in Christ over His entire creation."[22] The Kingdom of God was inaugurated through the life of Jesus Christ and has been actively involved in history. It continues to be involved today, and will be until it will be consummated upon His return and Final Judgment.

"When people receive Christ they are born again into his kingdom," begin the authors of the Lausanne Covenant. They "must seek not only to exhibit but also to spread its righteousness in the midst of an unrighteous world. The salvation we claim should be transforming us in the totality of our personal and social responsibilities."[23] As we live our lives in submission to Christ's reign, we are to oppose sin

22. "Amillennialism," accessed December 10, 2010, http://www.the-highway.com/amilc_Hoekema.html.

23. "The Lausanne Covenant," The Lausanne Movement, Accessed May 19, 2011, http://www.lausanne.org/covenant.

in every facet of our lives, not just our spiritual lives.[24] In a very practical sense, this means for Christians:

> Marriage should not be avoided by Christians, but sanctified. Emotions should not be repressed, but purified. Sexuality is not simply to be shunned, but redeemed. Politics should not be declared off-limits, but reformed. Art ought not to be pronounced worldly, but claimed for Christ. Business must no longer be relegated to the secular world, but must be made to conform again to God-honoring standards.[25]

It is in commitment to Christ and His Kingdom that we are to live our lives and have our sphere of influence.

Besides, based upon the trajectory of certain legislation, especially in the areas of sexual orientation and abortion, not being involved in the political process could do more to impede evangelistic efforts than being involved. If you don't believe me, just consider the following examples:

> In Massachusetts parents are not allowed to opt-out their children from homosexual related subjects, even for religious reasons. The reason parents are inhibited from making such decisions is because they would send a message of inferiority to students with same-sex parents.[26] According to Federal Judge Mark Wolf, the nor-

24. Wolters, *Creation Regained*, 73.

25 Ibid., 71.

26. "Parker v Hurley," United States District Court, accessed December 10, 2010, http://www.massresistance.org/docs/parker_lawsuit/motion_to_dismiss_2007/order_motion_to_dismiss_022307.pdf.

malization of homosexual behavior will prepare students to become "engaged and productive citizens in our democracy."[27]

Private Organizations, such as the Boy Scouts of America and the Christian Legal Society (CLS), are being challenged[28] and even denied the right to bar self-identified homosexuals from positions of leadership.[29]

Catholic Charities of Boston opted out of the adoption business since state law would have required them to place children in the homes of same-sex couples.[30]

A business owned and operated by Christians was fined more than $6,000 for refusing to photograph a lesbian commitment ceremony in New Mexico.[31]

Joseph Holland was arrested for praying the rosary in front of a Planned Parenthood facility within the limitations of the law. Besides, even

27. Ibid., 4–5.

28. "Boy Scouts of America et. al. *v.* Dale," FindLaw, accessed May 19, 2011, http://caselaw.lp.findlaw.com/scripts/getcase.pl?court=US&vol=000&invol=99-699.

29. "Christian Fellowship *v.* Martinez et al." Supreme Court of the United States, accessed December 10, 2010, http://www.supremecourt.gov/opinions/09pdf/08-1371.pdf.

30. "Banned in Boston," The Weekly Standard, accessed December 10, 2011, http://www.weeklystandard.com/Content/Public/Articles/000/000/012/191kgwgh.asp.

31. "Vanessa Willock *v.* Elane Photography." Human Rights Commission New Mexico, accessed December 10, 2010, http://media.npr.org/documents/2008/jun/photography.pdf.

> if he were breaking this particular law, to have arrested Joseph exceeds the penalties as established by that law.[32]
>
> An Augusta State University graduate student in the school of counseling—Jennifer Keaton -is currently suing the school for requiring her to undergo a remediation program to change her position on homosexual behavior and transgendered persons, or be expelled from the school.[33]
>
> Julea Ward, a student at Eastern Michigan University, was removed from the school's counseling program because she refused to counsel homosexual students on religious grounds.[34]

With legislation in the areas of abortion and sexual orientation affecting both public and private associations, it will only be a matter of time before churches are forbidden to speak out against homosexual behavior, which is already taking place in parts of Europe and Canada. If the government is permitted to censor the church in this way, what will stop it from censoring it in other ways? This is why not being involved in the political process will do more to inhibit evangelism than being involved will.

32. "Praying Outside Clinic," Fox News, accessed December 10, 2010, http://www.foxnews.com/us/2010/07/31/pub-chicago-man-charged-disorderly-conduct-praying-outside-planned-parenthood/.

33. "Lawsuit Claims," Fox News, accessed December 10, 2010, http://www.foxnews.com/us/2010/07/27/georgia-university-tells-student-lose-religion-lawsuit-claims/?test=faces.

34. "Court Upholds Expulsion," Fox News, accessed December 10, 2010, http://www.foxnews.com/us/2010/07/28/court-university-expel-student-opposes-homosexuality/.

INVOLVEMENT WITHIN THE DEMOCRATIC PROCESS FACILITATES EVANGELISM

Instead of impeding evangelistic efforts, it can be argued that our involvement within the political process actually facilitates evangelism. Voting, working with others on a particular issue, and joining associations will bring Christians into relationships with non-Christians. Relationships that are established around mutual causes will naturally facilitate evangelism when questions of motivation and purpose arise. In the end, to say that political involvement will impede evangelistic efforts is misleading since our involvement places us in the world where evangelism can actually occur.[35]

35. Mott, 124–25.

3

The Government's Role and Authority are Limited by God

LIKE ALL other governments, the American government is "established by God" (Rom 13.1) and possesses a limited authority delegated by God (John 19.10–11). Even though the American people created and now maintain our form of government by electing officials to serve within it, the government and those who serve her still possess a limited authority delegated by God. What we'll observe from Romans 13.1–7, with the support of other scriptures in the Old and New Testaments, is that governments and political parties are not to receive an "unqualified endorsement" for their existence, necessity, and authority is temporal[1] and delegated.[2]

1. Hart, *A Secular Faith,* 41.

2. Mott, 151. Douglas Moo commented, "From a human perspective, rulers come to power through force or heredity or popular choice. But the 'transformed mind' recognizes behind every such process the hand of God" (Moo, 798). John Eidsmoe observed, "In gleaning from the Lutheran tradition, Paul Sonnack noted that "The crucial thing is that we understand that the Christian is subject to secular authority for the sake of the neighbor, not for his or her own sake" (376). Consequently, Christians are to subject themselves to the governing authorities not only for the sake of God's authority,

THE GOVERNMENT'S AUTHORITY IS LIMITED, NOT FINAL

Every government's authority is limited, not final. There are two reasons why we can draw this conclusion from Romans 13.1–7.

First, after Paul encouraged his readers to subject themselves to the governing authorities in verse 1, he then explained to them that there "is no authority except from God, and those that exist have been instituted by God" (Rom 13.1). What we clearly observe in this verse is that "no authority" except that which is delegated by God exists and the governing authorities that do currently exist are "established" by God. Though governing authorities may come to power through an election or appointment, the Christian mind transformed by God's word is able to recognize that "behind every such process [is] the hand of God."[3] Thus, any and every form of government derives its authority from God and is limited by His parameters.

The second indication that the government's authority is limited is found in Romans 13.4 and 6, where we see that Paul carries along a continuous religious category in describing government officials as "ministers" and "servants of God." The various Greek terms used in these passages indicate that the work of governing authorities is a "religious function," especially *leitourgos*, which is typically translated as "ministers" in Romans 13.6. [4] However, we may want to

---

but also for the sake of their neighbor. For the know that government cannot exist without the obedience of its citizens" (Eidsmoe, 29).

3. Moo, 798.

4. Ibid., 804.

steer clear of emphasizing such a meaning since *leitourgos* "was used widely in Greek at the time to denote public officials of various kinds."[5] Nonetheless, any governing authority is considered to be serving on behalf of God.

With these two reasons in mind I believe we can readily agree with Leon Morris' comments on the limited role of the government and governing authorities:

> Paul's view is distinctive. He is firmly convinced that God is in control and that nobody secures a position of rulership unless God permits. Ordered government is not a human device, but something of divine origin. The servants of God must accordingly submit to its laws. Paul regards rulers not as autonomous, but as "established by God" (v. 1); the ruler is "God's servant" (v. 4). This gives the ruler a special dignity but at the same time stresses that his position is a subordinate one. He is to do, not whatever he wishes, but what the will of God is for him in his situation.[6]

Since the government and its officials, such as elected politicians, derive their authority from God, we can infer that their authority is limited and ultimately subjected to God's authority. This is why Stephen Mott said, "The authority of God, under which government functions, provides the basis for judging specific acts of governments."[7]

Not only does Romans 13.1–7 reveal this to us, but the entire corpus of Scripture, both Old and New Testaments, suggests this.

5. Ibid., 804.
6. Morris, 458.
7. Mott, 150.

THE OLD TESTAMENT

The limitation of government was not a new concept developed by Paul. Rather, this concept was inherited from his Jewish heritage and understanding of the Old Testament.[8] John Stott commented on Romans 13.1–7 that Paul "inherited a long-standing tradition from the Old Testament that Yahweh is sovereign over human kingdoms . . ."[9] Let us briefly consider several passages from the Old Testament that point to God's sovereign rule—which is His independent and self-governing rule—over the nations.

In the Book of Job, we read that God "makes nations great, and He destroys them; He enlarges nations, and leads them away" (Job 12.23; also see Isa 26.15). In Jeremiah 25.7–14 we observe that God has used one nation as a means of judgment against another (also see Isa 10.5–11).

We read in three different portions from Daniel "the Most High rules the kingdom of men and gives it to whom he will and sets over it the lowliest of men . . . the Most High rules the kingdom of men and gives it to whom he will . . ." (Dan 4.17, 25; cf. 4.32).

Finally—yet not conclusively—we read that Solomon declared that by God "kings reign, and rulers decree what is just" (Prov 8.15).

What these few passages indicate, as well as the general teaching of the Old Testament, is that God is sovereign and rules and reigns over the nations, both good and evil.[10]

8. Stott, 340.

9. Ibid., 340.

10. John Stott said, "We need to be cautious . . . in our interpretation of Paul's statements. He cannot be taken to mean that all [evil rulers]

It is from this foundation that Paul is working in Romans 13.1–7.[11]

THE NEW TESTAMENT

Romans 13.1–7 is not a standalone passage in the New Testament that addresses matters of civil government. In fact, this passage and others are based upon Jesus' teaching on the government. With this in mind, let us now turn our attention to Jesus' words.

The Gospels

In extracting Jesus' teachings on government, I want to avoid the tendency to isolate His teachings and use them to develop a position on civil government that calls for Christian disassociation with it. I would like to relate four reasons why I believe such a position is not tenable.

First, God has given us the entire Bible, both Old and New Testaments, as an infallible guide in glorifying and enjoying Him forever (2 Sam. 23.2; Matt. 15.6; Rom. 3.2; 2 Tim. 3.16–17; 1 Pet. 1.23; and 2 Pet. 1.20–21).[12] There is no legitimate reason for us to limit the teaching on government to the Gospels. Besides, even if we did we would be hard-pressed to develop a strict separatist position, which leads me to my next point.

---

were personally appointed by God, that God is responsible for their behavior, or that their authority is in no [way] to be resisted. Paul means [that] all human authority is [delegated by] God" (Stott, 340).

11. Moo, 794.

12. Williamson, *The Westminster Confession of Faith*, questions 1 and 2.

Second, Jesus Christ did not call for the disassociation of His followers from government. If anything, He legitimized the civil government's existence. Consider the following.

In an attempt to trap Jesus "in what he said" (Matt 22.15), the Pharisees and Herodians worked together in developing a plan (Matt 22.15–16). In an attempt to trap Jesus in His words, this group of Jewish men asked, "Is it lawful to pay taxes to Caesar, or not?" (Matt 22.17). It's interesting to note that the Pharisees and Herodians took different positions in regard to supporting the Roman government.[13]

Such a politically charged question as to the legitimacy of paying taxes could not have been better for the Pharisees and Herodians to work together in setting this philosophical trap. On one hand, the Pharisees did not support the Roman government and would have considered any tax not based upon the Torah unnecessary. On the other hand, the Heriodians might have been considered supporters of the Herodian dynasty who in turn supported the Roman government.[14] In commenting upon this passage, David Turner said: "The Jewish leaders evidently wish to catch Jesus in a dilemma. If he supports the tax, he will alienate the Pharisees, and if he rejects the tax, he will alienate the Herodians and be treasonous to Rome."[15] Amazingly, Jesus does neither.

> But Jesus, aware of their malice said, "Why put me to the test, you hypocrites? Show me the

13. Turner, *Matthew*, 527.
14. France, *The Gospel of Matthew*, 832.
15. Turner, 527.

> coin for the tax." And they brought him a denarius. And Jesus said to them, "Whose likeness and inscription is this?" They said, "Caesar's." Then he said to them, "Therefore render to Caesar the things that are Caesar's, and to God the things that are God's" (Matt 22.18–21; also see Mark 12.12).

In His response, Jesus supports neither the Pharisees nor the Herodians.[16] Instead, He strikes an amazing balance in affirming the legitimacy of government while maintaining allegiance to God. As in the words of John Piper, "Jesus has called for a kind of allegiance in two directions: to Caesar according to his ownership and authority, and to God according to his ownership and authority."[17] What is interesting to consider is what belongs to Caesar is limited, because everything belongs to God and He is the ultimate authority in every country, which means whatever authority the government has is subordinate to His (Dan 7.13–14; Matt 9.6; 11.27; John 3.35; 5.27; 17.2; Acts 2.36; Rom 14.9; 1 Cor 15.27; Eph 1.10, 20–22; Col 2.10; Phil 2.9; Heb 1.2; 2.8; 1 Pet 3.22).

What is more, Jesus implicitly affirmed the government and military personnel in Matthew 8.5–13. This passage of Scripture recounts the second of three subsequent healings in Matthew 8.1–17 involving a Centurion and his servant. At that time, a Centurion was a military official commanding a hundred soldiers.[18] Although the main thrust of this passage appears to be the comparison of faith

16. Ibid., 529.

17. Piper, *What Jesus Demands from the World*, 325.

18. Turner, 232.

with unbelief, it can be argued that if Jesus was a strict separatist He would have confronted the Centurion in His work rather than holding him up as a model of faith.

Third, to look solely to Jesus' teachings on piety and good works—such as the Sermon on the Mount - as a means of developing a position on the role of the civil government is to make a mistake in application. For example, in Matthew 5.38–42 Jesus declares:

> "You have heard that it was said, 'An eye for an eye and a tooth for a tooth.' But I say to you, Do not resist the one who is evil. But if anyone slaps you on the right cheek, turn to him the other also. And if anyone would sue you and take your tunic, let him have your cloak as well. And if anyone forces you to go one mile, go with him two miles. Give to the one who begs from you, and do not refuse the one who would borrow from you.

Reading this passage in isolation implies that there is no room for self-defense or the participation of Christians within law enforcement or military positions. On the surface this may be the case, but once we consider this passage in relationship to Jesus' teachings elsewhere in the Gospel of Matthew and the New Testament we can readily draw another conclusion.

Commenting upon the application of this very passage, Dr. David VanDrunen had the following to say:

> Jesus commends the great faith of a centurion (8:10), yet gives not the slightest hint that this faith is incompatible with his inherently violent occupation. Other places in the NT are

> similar (Acts 10:1–11:18). Later in Matthew the Pharisees give Jesus perfect opportunity to strip Caesar of his legitimate civil authority. But though Jesus strips Caesar of divine pretensions, he implicitly acknowledges his authority to levy taxes (enforcement of which requires the threat of coercion) (22:15–22). Elsewhere the NT affirms this authority much more explicitly (see Rom 13:1–7). The whole of Matthew's gospel, therefore, indicates that Jesus' prohibition of the lex talionis [law of retribution] in his kingdom does not mean the end of ordinary civil order or the end of his disciples' participation in the coercive enforcement of civil justice.[19]

What can be gleaned from Dr. VanDrunen is that every commandment of the Bible is not meant to be applied in isolation from its larger context, for the commandments of God can have multiple purposes, such as revealing our sin and need for forgiveness through faith in Jesus Christ (Gal 3.24), as a means of curtailing evil, and as a means of revealing what is both pleasing and offensive to God.[20]

Finally, Jesus' teachings on the state are the very foundation on which the other New Testament passages are built. His brief and simple teaching was readily embraced and elaborated on by His followers. Consider the following examples from the rest of the New Testament:

19. VanDrunen, "Bearing Sword in the State, Turning Cheek in the Church," accessed December 5, 2010, http://www.thegospelcoalition.org/publications/34-3/bearing-sword-in-the-state-turning-cheek-in-the-church.

20. Sproul, "The Threefold Use of the Law," Monergism, accessed December 15, 2010, http://www.monergism.com/thethreshold/articles/onsite/sproul/threefold_law.html.

> Be subject for the Lord's sake to every human institution, whether it be to the emperor as supreme, or to governors as sent by him to punish those who do evil and to praise those who do good. For this is the will of God, that by doing good you should put to silence the ignorance of foolish people. Live as people who are free, not using your freedom as a cover-up for evil, but living as servants of God. Honor everyone. Love the brotherhood. Fear God. Honor the emperor (1 Pet. 2.13–17).

> First of all, then, I urge that supplications, prayers, intercessions, and thanksgivings be made for all people, for kings and all who are in high positions, that we may lead a peaceful and quiet life, godly and dignified in every way (1 Tim 2.1–2).

> Remind them to be submissive to rulers and authorities, to be obedient, to be ready for every good work (Titus 3.1).

What all of these passages suggest "is that Jesus' teaching about the relationship of the disciple to the state was the basis for a widespread early Christian tradition, which Paul here takes up and adapts."[21] This is why many have concluded that Jesus' teaching on His disciples' relationship to the state was widespread in early Christian tradition.[22]

Though the limited role and responsibility of the government imposed by God may appear to be a theologically

21. Moo, 793.
22. Ibid., 793.

abstract position, it bears tremendous implications for us today. Consider the following three points.

WHAT DOES THIS MEAN FOR THE UNITED STATES?

First, as Christians we have a duty to God above and beyond the government. On one hand, we have an obligation to be submitted to the government authorities of the United States of America (Rom. 13.1); on the other hand, our duty to honor God supersedes our obligations to everyone and everything, even the government.[23] This point is further explained in "To Be, or Not to Be," but it is important to emphasize here that as Christians our primary purpose in life is to glorify God and enjoy Him forever.[24] The Scriptures are replete with such calls to glorify God in everything that we do (Exod 18.16; 20.3; Deut 10.20; John 19.11; Rom 11.36; 1 Cor 6.20; 8.6; 10.31; Col 1.16; Rev 4.11). Perhaps the best example of this is Peter's response to being asked to stop teaching in the name of Jesus - "We must obey God rather than men" (Acts 5.27–29; cf. 4.19–20).

Second, governments are ordained by God with a specific role and purpose. As previously eluded to, governments have the responsibility of maintaining order, promoting the common good, providing for our defense, and protecting the freedoms of each and every citizen.[25]

23. Mott, 151.

24. Williamson, shorter catechism 1.1.

25. Corwin Smidt brilliantly said, "While God has given the state a separate sphere of authority, its responsibilities do not involve doing the work of the Church. In other words, the state is not to be an agent for the propagation of religion or the securing of salvation.

Within the realm of civil society the government has a difficult role in maintaining order through promoting the common good and upholding justice while not overtly interfering in the realm of other institutions within society. "To have a Christian perspective on governments and the public policies they adopt," begins Steve Monsma, "it is important to understand that American society—as any society—is made up of more than the government and individuals." He goes on to say:

> Liberals tend to focus on government and its society-wide public policies; conservatives tend to focus on free individuals operating in a free market. Both can forget there is much more to society than the government and individuals. A host of social institutions and organizations lies between government and the individual: families, churches, nonprofit organizations, self-help groups, recreation clubs, sports leagues, art organizations, voluntary associations, and many more.[26]

In striking such a balance, Monsma recommends that public policies should respect, make room for, and make use

---

Rather, through God's graciousness to all people, he has granted the institution of the state to care for the common interests and general welfare of the people over which it has authority. Here the distinction between particular and common grace sharpens our understanding of the role of the state; it is an agency of common, not particular grace. Government's role is the mitigation of evil in a fallen world, not the redemption of human sinful nature. Its tasks are not to redeem its citizens but to sustain the created order. The role of the state is specific and practical; it must maintain the law and uphold the public justice" (Corwin Smidt, *Church, State and Public Justice*, 145).

26. Monsma, *Healing for a Broken World*, 79–80.

of the institutions of civil society. They should be actively involved when matters of justice and the common good require it, and policies should reflect differences of opinion and diversity on the local, state, and federal levels.[27]

Third, not only is our government's roles and responsibilities limited, but the very necessity of its existence and authority is temporal. According to Daryl Hart, author of *Secular Faith*, not grasping this reality has become the "Achilles heel of many Christian politicians." He goes on to say that many have failed to "recognize the impermanence of secular politics, that it is a temporary arrangement to restrain evil and promote justice until the dawn of a new period in the history of salvation."[28] This is why no one—especially Christians—should overtly place faith, hope, and trust in what any government can accomplish.

Unfortunately some have fallen victim to placing an excessive dependence upon political reform and have used excessive power and ungodly tactics in ascertaining their position. This is one of the major reasons why some Christians deny political involvement or speak against those who are involved.

Although such instances have blackened the eye of Christianity in certain respects, they do not merit Christians retracting from obeying the will of God in submitting to our form of government. Commenting in a similar vein of thought, Daryl Hart said, "Even though the politics of the earthly city may proceed from selfishness or irreligious motivation, its authority is still legitimate and something in

27. Ibid., 88–92.

28. Hart, 41.

which believers may participate."[29] So, regardless of the actions committed by some both yesterday and today, in the eyes of God the government still maintains a legitimate role to which we are called to submit (Rom 13.1).

In light of historical and contemporary mistakes we can move forward with important lessons to better guide our involvement within the political process.

MOVING FORWARD FROM HISTORICAL AND CONTEMPORARY MISTAKES

What we learn from yesterday's mistakes is this all-important lesson: humility. I'm not saying that Christians are to act in a state of insignificance or inferiority, but rather in an attitude of modesty and self-appraisal. As in the words of James Skillen:

> We must constantly act with an attitude of true humility. We should undertake every civic duty, every political action . . . with the avowed understanding that they are not God's will but only our response to God's will . . . This attitude of humility will lead us to be modest and self-critical in our claims and stated intentions.[30]

In a similar vein of thought, Steve Monsma and Mark Rogers said:

> But history also teaches Christians to move into active political engagement only after careful reflection and much prayer. This is not an area

29. Ibid., 41.
30. Smidt, 147.

> to rush into with maximum of enthusiasm and good intentions and a minimum of thought and planning.[31]

History teaches us that Christian's involvement within the democratic process should be marked with a high level of humility and reflection.[32] Not only do the lessons of history lead us to such a conclusion, so too does the difficulty of applying basic principles of the Bible to contemporary policies and situations.[33]

As Christians we are not to be plagued with a high level of inactivity; we are simply to move forward with a high level of humility, love, and empathy. In clearer words, "Do nothing from rivalry or conceit, but in humility count others more significant than yourselves. Let each of you look not only to his own interests, but also to the interests of others" (Phil 2.3–4). Such an attitude is pleasing to God (1 Pet 3.4) and considered the pathway to honor within His Kingdom (Prov 16.18). Perhaps this is why St. Augustine of Hippo considered the three greatest virtues to be "Humility, humility, and then humility."

31. Monsma and Rogers, *Toward an Evangelical Public Policy*, 326.

32. Ibid., 329.

33. Ibid., 329.

4

What's Love Got to Do With It?

The Working Out of Love Within the Political Process

When contending for the involvement of Christians within the democratic process in America, we have to address the unfortunate reality that many people under the guise of Christianity have been violent, mean-spirited, and downright nasty toward the very people for whom God sent His Son to die, people with whom He has called us to share the Gospel within the political realm in both word and deed.

For example, the bombing of abortion clinics and picketing the funerals of homosexuals with signs that say, "God Hates Fags"[1] are not actions done in love. This is not the way that Christians are called to submit to the government (Rom 13.1) and engage in the political process. Those who claim to be serving Jesus Christ and furthering His kingdom with such malice are misguided and wrong. Our submission to and involvement in the government and political process are to be in love.

1. Westboro Baptist Church, http://www.godhatesfags.com/.

As Christians we have much to learn about engaging the democratic process in love. If our political engagement is carried out in a way that does not reflect the love of God as expressed in Jesus Christ, then we run the risk of irreparably damaging the bridge between Christians and non-Christians. In fact, much damage has already been done.

From the research of The Barna Group, David Kinnaman and Gabe Lyons commented:

> Christians need to be aware of their reputation in this [political] arena, not only because it influences their political engagement, but because it affects their ability to connect with new generations who are innately skeptical of people who appear to use political power to protect their interests and viewpoints. This perception may not always be accurate, but it contributes to outsiders' mistrust of Christians.[2]

Although we have seen both Christians and non-Christians call for the privatization of religion, most people are not concerned with Christian involvement per se, "but they disagree with our methods and our attitudes."[3]

From their research, Kinnaman and Lyons observed among those polled that Christians:

> . . . seem to be pursuing an agenda that benefits only ourselves; they assert that we expect too much out of politics; they question whether we are motivated by our economic status rather than faith perspectives when we support conservative politics; they claim we act and say things

2. Kinnaman and Lyons, *UnChristian*, 157.

3. Ibid., 156.

> in an unchristian manner; they wonder where Jesus would use political power as we do; and they are concerned that we overpower the voices of other groups.[4]

Our love of God not only compels us to be faithful to Him, but drives us to love our neighbor, irrespective of his or her religious expression or political ideology (Matt 22.37–40; cf. Lev 19.18; Deut 6.5; Luke 10.27).

With this in mind we need to examine the context of Romans 13.1–7 and observe how a theme of love is woven throughout. Afterwards, we will consider how love is to be worked out within the political process.

THE FABRIC OF LOVE IN THE LARGER CONTEXT OF ROMANS 13.1–7

Leading up to our passage of study, Paul spent a considerable amount of time emphasizing acts of selfless love in Romans 12.9–21,[5] culminating in his affirmation, "Do not be overcome by evil, but overcome evil with good" (Rom 12.21). What does this have to do with Romans 13.1–7? Due to the "specific verbal cross-references" of Romans 12.9–21 and Romans 13.1–7,[6] these passages must be read as one

4. Ibid., 155–156.

5. Neufeld, "Submission to Governing Authorities," 93; and Yoder, *The Politics of Jesus*, 196.

6. Yoder, 197. John Howard Yoder added that "[Romans] 13.8 begins with a verbal echo of verse 7 . . . [and] the submission to the powers in 13.1 is motivated and exposited by the hope in 13.11–14. Verse 10, by expositing verse 8, also gives a definition of the 'good' in verse 3, whereby the behavior of Christians under government is guided."

continuous whole and not two separate passages.[7] In view of this we can reason that Paul's emphasis on selfless love is to be carried out in our relationship with the government.[8]

THE LOVE OF GOD WOVEN THROUGHOUT ROMANS 13

Romans 13 possesses a common thread of love woven throughout it. It's unfortunate that our English Bibles do not show the comparison between Romans 13.7 and 8. For instance, the words "render to all what is due" in verse 7 and "owe" in verse 8 come from the same root word, *opheilo*. So this means that verse 7 and 8 could be read like this:

> Verse 7: "Pay to all what is *owed* . . ." and
>
> Verse 8: "*Owe* no one anything, except to love each other . . ."[9]

We not only submit to the government by paying taxes and engaging in the democratic process, but we are to submit to the government, those who serve within it, and each and every citizen in America in love.

We are told by Paul in the rest of verse 8 that "the one who loves another has fulfilled the law." And at the end of verse 9 and all of 10 we are told that everything we do is summed up in these two sayings: "You shall love your neighbor as yourself" and "Love does no wrong to

7. Ibid., 196.

8. Since I am contending for the involvement of Christians within the Democratic Process, I am choosing not to address the topic of the involvement of Christians in wars sanctioned by the government.

9. Ibid., 196.

a neighbor; therefore love is the fulfilling of the law." As Christians, we are to love others as we love ourselves (Lev 19.18; Matt 22.39; Mark 12.31; Luke 10.27; Gal 5.14; Jas 2.8). This manner of love does no wrong to our neighbor (Rom 13.10), even through public policies. The love of God and our neighbor—all people—is the fulfillment of everything God requires of us (Gal 5.14; 6.2).

As we engage the political process, we are to do so in love; we are to speak the truth, but in love; we are to hold the government accountable for its actions, but in love. The standard of love that we use in judging all of our actions is the standard that Jesus Christ set by humbly sacrificing Himself for us on the cross.[10] "And as vigorously as the evangelical presses his battle," remarked Carl F.H. Henry, "he ought to be counted upon to point to the redemption that is in Christ Jesus as the only adequate solution."[11]

How, on a practical level, does this work out in the democratic process?

LOVE DETERMINES HOW WE ARE INVOLVED

Love determines how we are involved within the democratic process. Love for our neighbor will drive us beyond our own self-interests to seek the justice and common good for everyone in our community, state, and nation.[12] According to Dr. R. Albert Mohler Jr., President of the Southern Baptist Theological Seminary, "A Christian's motivation for entering the public square and advocating public policy is

10. Kinnaman and Lyons, 167.
11. Henry, *The Uneasy Conscience of Modern Fundamentalism*, 78.
12. Monsma, *Healing for a Broken World*, 74.

love of neighbor. Our concern in political, moral, social, and cultural engagement is not to impose Christianity . . . Rather, our concern is love for our neighbor. We are motivated by love for other human beings, believing that health and welfare and happiness and commonwealth are dependent on society's being ordered in such a way that the Creator's intentions for human relationships are honored and upheld—and that will inevitably require restrictions on human conduct."

Take the issue of abortion for example.

The love of our neighbor not only compels us to be a voice for the unborn child, but such love should compel us to seek the wellbeing of women who face difficult pregnancies or financial hardships in bringing their unborn child into the world.[13]

Even though the government does assist those in need financially, we must not allow the government's role to abdicate our own personal responsibility as followers of Christ in meeting the needs of those who are in such predicaments.

Economic factors do play a large role in determining a woman's or couple's choice in aborting their unborn child.[14] I've heard examples of families taking out a second mortgage on their home in order to provide the finances necessary to avoid an abortion. This is a great example of an act of love on behalf of others, both born and unborn.

13. Ibid., 118 and 122.

14. "Reducing Abortion in America," Catholics United, accessed December 10, 2010, http://www.nd.edu/~cdems/College_Democrats_of_Notre_Dame/College_Democrats_of_Notre_Dame/Issues_files/reducing-abortion-in-america.pdf.

This principal of solidarity—the love of our neighbor—is worked out in a myriad of ways. Steve Monsma, Senior Research Fellow at the Henry Institute for the Study of Christianity and Politics at Calvin College, explained how this principle of solidarity works itself out in practice:

> Sometimes solidarity will drive us to our knees in prayer, sometimes to giving our money to organizations offering help in Christ's name, sometimes to direct, personal acts of comfort and help, and sometimes to supporting public policies that oppose wrongs and promote greater justice. And sometimes it will lead us to pursue all four together.[15]

The love of our neighbor not only determines how we are involved in the democratic process; it also determines the manner in which we are involved.

THE MANNER IN WHICH CHRISTIANS ARE INVOLVED

Based upon my own unscientific observations, I am not at all surprised by the findings of David Kinnaman and Gabe Lyons whose research revealed that "Christians do not respect leaders whose political viewpoint is different from their own."[16] Without doing extensive research I think many will readily agree with their conclusion.

Based upon Kinnaman's and Lyon's research, it appears that the manner in which Christians are engaged in the political process is more influenced by talk show

15. Monsma, 76.

16. Ibid., 169.

radio hosts than the Scriptures.[17] I think it's important for all of us to remember that politics do not supersede God, nor replace our confession of faith and life in Jesus Christ. Just because we are talking about political matters doesn't mean that our involvement and manner of conduct is compartmentalized from our faith. So, regardless of someone's political affiliation, we are commanded to love and pray for our leaders - not for their death and eternal damnation,[18] but for their wellbeing, so that we may lead a peaceful life. It is this attitude and behavior that is good and pleasing to God (1 Tim 2.1–3).

Even though we may disagree with others on a host of political issues, such as taxation, healthcare, immigration, marriage, and abortion to name a few, these disagreements do not give us the right to disrespect, degrade, or debase those with whom we disagree. Regardless of a civil servants political position, we are to pay him or her respect. We see this exemplified in the Old Testament and clarified in the New Testament.

In the Old Testament Book of Exodus, we read a series of laws concerning social justice (Exod 22.16–31). What I would like to pay particular attention to is Exodus 22.28, which reads, "You shall not curse God, nor curse a ruler of your people" (Exod 22.28; cf. 1 Sam. 24.7, 11; 26.23;

17. When referencing the Scriptures I am referencing the Bible, which is considered the Word of God and is made up of both the Old and New Testaments. The Bible is the only standard that God has given us in directing us how we are to glorify and enjoy Him (see The Westminster Shorter Catechism Q and A 2).

18. "Phoenix Pastor Draws Protests," Fox News, accessed December 10, 2010, http://www.foxnews.com/politics/2009/08/31/phoenix-pastor-draws-protests-telling-church-prays-obamas-death/.

Eccl. 8.2–5; 10.20). The first facet of this verse, "You shall not curse God," is a recapitulation of an earlier command in this series of verses, namely Exodus 22.20. Now, what is important for us is what immediately follows: "nor curse a ruler of your people." Not only are we not to curse God, but we are not to curse those in positions of authority, whether they are parents, teachers, police officers, or civil magistrates. The appearance of these statements in the very same sentence indicates the importance placed on not cursing a ruler of the people. In other words, cursing your leader is second only to cursing God.

Consider the example set by Daniel, Shadrach, Meshach, and Abednego (Dan 1.7). These men were commanded to eat and drink of the king's choice food and wine (Dan 1.5, 8). However, the foods provided by King Nebuchadnezzar would have caused these Jewish men to break the Mosaic dietary laws as established in Leviticus 1, and therefore cause them to sin against God. In choosing to honor God, these four Jewish men refused to eat the king's food, but they did so in a loving manner.

Commenting upon this passage, John MacArthur said:

> It is important to note that, even while refusing to do what God had forbidden, those four faithful men of God showed respect for the human authority they had to disobey. Speaking for the other three as well as for himself, Daniel did not demand deference to their beliefs but respectfully "sought permission from the commander of the officials that he might not defile himself"

> (v. 8), and he referred to themselves as the commander's "servants" (vv. 12–13).[19]

These four men did not act in a "Holier than Thou" mentality, disrespectfully condemning the civil authority's actions as an abomination.

Daniel exhibited a similar attitude again later. A Babylonian king by the name of Darius enacted a policy that punished anyone who prayed to another god besides the king himself, by throwing the offender into the lion's den (Dan 6.6–9). Once again Daniel refused to obey this policy because it would have caused him to sin against the commandment of God to "have no others gods before Me" (Exod 20.3). Once again, MacArthur points out Daniel's demeanor:

> Daniel respectfully but firmly refused to obey the decree. . .it is important to note Daniel's lack of malice and his genuine respect for the human authority his conscience forced him to disobey. After being released unharmed, he said 'O king, live forever!' (v. 21).[20]

In spite of being placed into a position of potential compromise, Daniel—and the other three Jewish men—set an example for us in the manner of love that we are to exhibit in our dealings with the governing authorities.

At this point some will argue, "But that was for the Old Testament and has no bearing for today." But does it? This point exemplified in the Old Testament is clarified in the New Testament. In the New Testament Book of Acts, we

19. MacArthur, *Daniel*, 215.

20. Ibid., 215.

see the command of Exodus 22.28 quoted and exemplified by the Apostle Paul. In this historical recollection, we read of an account of the Apostle Paul standing on trial before the Jewish Supreme Court, the Sanhedrin (Acts 23). After affirming the manner that he has lived his life, the Jewish high priest, Ananias, ordered those standing beside Paul to strike him on the mouth (Acts 23.2). In response, Paul vociferously declared, "God is going to strike you, you white-washed wall! Do you sit to try me according to the Law, and in violation of the Law order me to be struck?" (Acts 23.3). The bystanders standing around informed him that the one he was speaking to was in fact the high priest (Acts 23.4). Becoming aware of whom he was speaking to, Paul quoted the commandment just referenced above, saying, "I was not aware, brethren, that he was high priest; for it is written, 'YOU SHALL NOT SPEAK EVIL OF A RULER OF YOUR PEOPLE'" (Acts 25.5).

Although the Jewish high priest wrongfully commanded those by Paul to strike him in the mouth, this did not nullify Paul from personal responsibility in not speaking evil against the ruler of God's people.

There have been times and there will be times when Christians will be wrongfully accused of crimes, wrongfully sued, and wrongfully judged. This doesn't give us the right or privilege to act in any manner we see fit, especially if it is compartmentalized from the Gospel.

As we look to Christ, who left the comforts of heaven and descended to earth to be born as a human baby in a manger, we will see that our manner toward others should be marked with a high-level of humility. We see this no more clearly than in the Book of Philippians:

> Do nothing from rivalry or conceit, but in humility count others more significant than yourselves. Let each of you look not only to his own interests, but also to the interests of others. Have this mind among yourselves, which is yours in Christ Jesus (Phil 2.3–5).

This manner of life will compel us to leave the comfort of our own peer group to engage in conversations with those who differ in opinion. The advice of Kinnaman and Lyons is very pertinent when they asked, "What are you doing to facilitate conversations with people you don't agree with? Just asking what they think about certain issues, without having an 'agenda' to change their mind, might shift their perceptions of you."[21] Such an attitude exemplified by Christians may best lead to true bipartisan politics that leads us to finding solutions to common problems and concerns.

21. Kinnaman and Lyons, 169.

5

Maintaining Order

The Government's Role in Encouraging Good Behavior and Discouraging Bad Behavior

IN ROMANS 13.1–7, Paul summarizes[1] two main reasons why followers of Jesus Christ are to be submitted to the governing authorities: wrath and conscience. These two reasons are found in Paul's summarization of verses 1–4 in Romans 13.5: "Therefore one must be in subjection, not only to avoid God's wrath but also for the sake of conscience." These two principles provide Christians with a balanced approach in submitting to the governing authorities in the United States of America.

What we will briefly observe below is that governments are primarily assigned the task of maintaining order by encouraging good behavior and discouraging bad behavior.

MAINTAIN ORDER

To the dismay of many, the purpose of government reaches far beyond taxation, regulation, law enforcement,

1. Moo, 803.

and political parties.[2] Within certain Christian traditions, such as the Reformed tradition, the government possesses a positive role in the lives of Christians and non-Christians alike. Not only are governments given the charge of punishing bad conduct (Rom 13.3–4), they are also responsible for creating an environment by which men and women of any race and religion can work together for the common good.[3] This positive role of the government is maintained by pointing out that governments did not derive from sin, but rather originated in the outworking of creation by mankind.

Genesis 1.1–27 describes the beginning and end of God's creation, but not the end of creation's development.[4] In further developing God's good creation (Gen 1.31), mankind was given the mandate to multiply, subdue the earth (i.e. develop the earth's resources), work, and exercise great care over the earth (Gen 1.28; 2.15). In the words of Albert Wolters, "People must now carry on the work of development: by being fruitful they must fill it even more; by subduing it they must form it even more. Mankind, as God's representatives on earth, carries on where God left off."[5] It is this continual development of creation by mankind from which the idea of government springs.[6]

You see, even if sin never entered into the world through the disobedience of Adam and Eve (Gen 3.1–7,

2. Eidsmoe, 3.

3. Smidt, 131.

4. Wolters, 43.

5. Ibid., 41. Also see Van Til, *The Calvinistic Concept of Culture*, 29; Monsma, 33–34.

6. Smidt, 130.

17; Rom 5.12–19; 8.20–22), government would have likely developed as the human race continued to multiply in number and developed the earth's resources for useful purposes.[7] Even within a sinless world, some form of government would have been necessary to maintain order. It is with this understanding that Steve Monsma observed:

> There would have had to have been some means to create rules that would have made it possible for human societies to develop and for people in them to live together in order and harmony. There would have had to have been a way to regulate trade and commerce, probably including the creation of money, a way to decide jointly where cities should be located and to organize the different sections of the cities, and, once automobiles had been invented, something as simple as deciding on which side of the roads people should drive. Even in a sinless world, as human beings developed all the possibilities God had placed in his creation, some society-wide policies would have to have been established.[8]

From this foundation a positive role of the government is developed in the outworking of creation by mankind.

In maintaining societal order, there are two broad principles that we glean from Romans 13.3–4 by which governments are to secure such order: encouraging good behavior

7. This thought was elaborated by Van Til, who said, "Culture, then, is any and all human effort and labor expended upon the cosmos, to unearth its treasures and its riches and bring them into the service of man for the enrichment of human existence unto the glory of God" (Van Til, 29–30).

8. Monsma, 36.

and discouraging bad behavior.[9] In writing these words to the Church in Rome around 56 AD, Paul would have subverted the contemporary understanding of government. That is, the government during this time would have operated from a hierarchical perspective, seeking the good of the government and government officials, not the people.

ENCOURAGING THE GOOD

In Romans 13.3, we read: "For rulers are not a terror to good conduct, but to bad." In determining the meaning of "good" (*agathos*) "conduct" (*ergon*) there has been a few suggestions made.[10] Once we juxtapose use of the term in verses 3–4 of this passage, we'll observe that Paul has in mind one clear meaning: morality.

The meaning of *agathos* is defined as "the good, what is good, right; what is intrinsically valuable, morally good."[11] This meaning is further clarified when we observe its usage in Romans 13.3–4.

First, we observe a contrast in good behavior and evil. We see this in Rom. 13.3 when we read that we are not to be fearful of government officials for "good behavior, but for evil."

Second, this point is clarified in Romans 13.4. We observe in principle that governments should not punish or discourage good behavior but rather encourage it.[12] What is

9. Moo, 800.
10. Morris, 463–64.
11. Bauer, 3.
12. Morris, 464.

more, we also see this point contrasted by the government's role in punishing evil behavior (more on this later).

There are a few practical ways that our government can encourage good behavior from citizens of the United States.

First, government leaders are not to be self-serving, but to serve the public good. We see this clearly enunciated in Romans 13.3–4 which reads, "Do what is good and you will have praise from the same; for it [the government] is a minister of God to you for good."[13] Commenting upon this passage more than 400 years ago, John Calvin pithily said:

> Magistrates may hence learn what their vocation is, for they are not to rule for their own interest, but for the public good; nor are they endued with unbridled power, but what is restricted to the wellbeing of their subjects; in short, they are responsible to God and to men in the exercise of their power.[14]

What Calvin wisely observed is that governments and governmental leaders are to be restricted by the public good and the wellbeing of the people they represent.

Second, governments can encourage good behavior through legislation. God has given governments the authority to create laws for the purpose of maintaining order in society. Laws cannot create good people, but they can encourage good decisions.[15] Laws have an educative factor

13. The *New American Standard Bible.*

14. "Commentary on Romans," John Calvin, accessed December 5, 2010, http://www.ccel.org/ccel/calvin/calcom38.xvii.ii.html.

15. Pendleton, *American Values*, 191.

and influence the decisions that people make.[16] For instance, marriages are "an important social good, associated with an impressively broad array of positive outcomes for children and adults alike" [17] that have a penetrating effect upon the well-being of any society. [18] Governments can encourage, support, and even protect marriages through legislation that provides spousal benefits and discourages marital dissolution by limiting its recognizable grounds.

Finally, governments can encourage good behavior by praising it. Though governments are better known for enforcing the law and punishing criminal behavior, they do possess a role in "fostering virtue and service."[19] In teasing out suggestions in how governments can go about fostering good behavior by praising it, John Stott writes:

> Most countries also have some arrangement for recognizing those of their citizens who have made a conspicuous contribution to the public good. They give them a citation or a certificate, a title, a decoration or some other token of appreciation. But they could probably improve and extend their award system, so that only outstanding merit is rewarded, and their honours become increasingly prized and coveted, like the international Nobel and Templeton awards. Perhaps

16. Mott, 205.

17. "Can Government Strengthen Marriage?" Institute for American Values, accessed December 5, 2010, http://www.marriagedebate.com/pdf/Can%20Government%20Strengthen%20Marriage.pdf.

18. For the incomparable importance of the familial institution upon men, women, children, and society, see Gallagher, *The Case for Marriage*.

19. Stott, 346.

> citizens should be given stronger encouragement to recommend people from their community for public recognition.[20]

Such practical steps in praising good behavior would go a long way in encouraging citizens to conduct good deeds in their community.

DISCOURAGE THE BAD

Though varying opinions have been made as to the role of the government in discouraging bad behavior, it has been widely accepted that governments have been given authority by God to carry out a punitive function.[21] The notion of "wrath" (*orge*)—as found in Romans 13.5—denotes "vengeance and punishment."[22] Since this verse serves as a summarization of verses 3–4,[23] we see that the meaning of "wrath" is the punitive function of the government. Look at verses 3–4:

> For rulers are not a cause of fear for good behavior, but for evil. Do you want to have no fear of authority? Do what is good and you will have praise from the same; for it is a minister of God to you for good. But if you do what is evil, be afraid; for it does not bear the sword for nothing;

20. Ibid., 346.

21. Morris, 464.

22. Mounce, *The Analytical Lexicon to the Greek New Testament*, 341.

23. Moo, 803.

> for it is a minister of God, an avenger who brings
> wrath on the one who practices evil.[24]

Not only are governments to be structured to encourage and reward good behavior, governments are also endowed with the authority to maintain societal order by punishing those "who practice evil" (cf. 1 Pet 2.13–14).[25] Understanding that governments have been given this role and responsibility is an important distinction to keep in mind.

As Christians and consequently the church, we are to live according to the precepts of love, not justice, whereas governments are to live according to justice, not love.[26] This distinction in roles and responsibilities between the state and church leave us with two very important observations.

First, as Christians we are called to cling to what is good (Rom 12.9), not repay evil with evil (Rom 12.17), to overcome evil with good (Rom 12.21), and not to seek revenge, but to leave room for the wrath of God (Rom 12.19).[27] If we are under threat for our faith in Jesus Christ or for being members of a particular church, then in the face of such persecution a "non-retaliation to aggression is an appropriate response according to Matthew 5.38–42" (cf. Matt 5.10–11)[28]

24. The *New American Standard Bible.*

25. The "evil" (*kakos*) spoken of hear is not an abstract thought or theory. The evil spoken of here is the very evil that God Himself condemns as such. For governments to exercise justice is an expression of God's wrath.

26. Stott, 345. Also see Moo, 800–801.

27. Ibid., 345.

28. VanDrunen, "Bearing Sword in the State, Turning Cheek in the Church," 334.

Second, as citizens of the United States of America we are permitted the same due process that non-Christian citizens are. That is, we are able to appeal to civil authorities over civil matters. Not only is this observed in understanding our submission to the existing form of government, but this is also observed in the example set by the early Apostles (Acts 22.25–29).[29]

Although governments have and will continue to abuse their authoritative roles and responsibilities, the fact that they are endowed with such authority is a good thing. This is why I believe we would do well to heed the words of John Calvin, who said that this passage reminds us that "it is through the divine goodness that they are defended by the sword of princes against injuries done by the wicked."[30]

In maintaining such societal order, we must understand that God has given governments the authority to create laws for the purpose of maintaining order in society. Even if we lived in a sinless era, governments would have to had possessed a level of authority to ensure that people under their influence would follow the law, thus ensuring coherent order.[31] Although sin has entered the hearts of mankind and this world and its governments are not as they should be (Gen 2.16–17; 2 Chr 6.36; Ps 51.5; 58.3; 143.2; Eccl 7.29; Mic 7.2–4; Mark 10.18; 1 Cor 15.21–22; Rom 3.23; 5.12, 18; Eph 2.1–3, 12; 4.18; Col 1.21; 2.13), this doesn't mean that we have the right to avoid governmental affairs on the federal, state, and local levels as if they were an

29. Ibid., 334.

30. "Commentary on Romans," John Calvin, accessed December 5, 2010, http://www.ccel.org/ccel/calvin/calcom38.xvii.ii.html.

31. Smidt, 130.

evil to be avoided. As said before, we have as much of a role and responsibility in the shaping of our great nation as non-Christians. Christians should be all the more compelled to influence our government to become "more in line with God's" original good intentions.[32]

YOU CAN'T LEGISLATE MORALITY

There are many who will cringe as they read over my last point. Besides, doesn't everyone agree that "You can't legislate morality?" On the surface this sounds like a compelling and reasonable argument. However, once we dig beneath this convincing rhetoric, I believe we will discover this position is based upon faulty reasoning, because nearly every law has a moral underpinning.

From Garrett DeWeese and J. P. Moreland's *Philosophy Made Slightly Less Difficult*, we see this point clearly enunciated:

> It is often said that you can't legislate morality. But in fact virtually all legislation is based on some moral principle. Traffic laws? A well-ordered traffic flow reduces injuries and deaths, and to seek such a reduction is a morally praiseworthy goal. Criminal law? Virtually all criminal law rests on moral principles such as "do not steal," "do not lie" and "do not kill." Tax law? Given that some government is necessary for a peaceful, well-functioning society, and given that government costs money, even tax law can, at least in theory, be traced to moral principles. Now some laws are matters of convenience rather than

32. Monsma, 36.

> morality (e.g., laws regulating the size, shape and weight of letters which can be mailed without excess postage). And some laws codify prudential or pragmatic judgments rather than moral principles (e.g., laws prohibiting parking at certain times along a street to allow for street sweeping). Still, for the most part, law and morality go far together, so that in most cases a lawbreaker is also morally blameworthy for the act.[33]

The very foundation of public policy and civil law is based upon some level of morality that implies what someone should and should not do. This holds true for conservatives and liberals, theist and non-theists, and Christians and non-Christians. What I hear when someone responds with the "you can't legislate morality" argument is that we can't encourage or pass legislation that is based upon a Christian worldview, just their personal views.

So the next time someone says, "You can't legislate morality," simply ask, "Why not?" I imagine they'll have a hard time explaining why Christians shouldn't impose their views without imposing their own secular views.[34]

Laws are concerned with what is right and wrong and are inherently religious in nature. Consequently, when discussing public policy, "the question is not which view is religious and which is purely rational; the question is which is true and which is false."[35]

33. DeWeese and Moreland, *Philosophy Made Slightly Less Difficult*, 84.

34. Beckwith and Koukl, *Relativism*, 144–45.

35. Pearcy, *Total Truth*, 42.

If we are to submit to the government out of fear of punishment, what if the government passed a law forbidding Christians from meeting publicly together? What if our government passed a planned birth policy, as in China, where people are coerced and even forced to submit to the law through bribery, forced sterilization, abortion, and possibly infanticide?[36] What if the there were a law passed forbidding people from spanking their children, like in Sweden and Finland?[37] Do we have to obey laws that forbid what God commands out of the fear of "wrath"? This question is answered by the second reason we are to submit to the governing authorities of the United States: for conscience sake.

36. "One-Child Policy," Wikipedia, accessed May 19, 2011, http://en.wikipedia.org/wiki/One-child_policy#Human_rights.

37. In further teasing out this point, Andreas Kostenberger's remarked, "A debate exists also over the use of physical punishment (spanking) as a valid or appropriate means for parents to discipline their children . . . Should parents exercise physical discipline? The modern criticisms against spanking typically employ overstatement and inflammatory rhetoric. Appealing to excessive cases that involve abuse does not justify abandoning spanking as a form of discipline. Children need to learn the consequences of wrong behavior, and spanking can be a useful means to convey that lesson. However, parents should take their child's unique personality and temperament into account and be aware that some children may respond better to alternative forms of positive or negative consequences and reinforcement (i.e., timeout, rewards, loss of privileges)" (Kostenberger, *God Marriage, and Family*, 157–59).

6

To Be, or Not to Be

Living Faithfully to Jesus Christ in the Public Square

THE SECOND overarching reason that we are to submit to the governing authorities is for the sake of conscience (*suneidesin*). Generally, our conscience is our sense of right and wrong that guides us in our decision making. Our conscience according to Romans 13.5, is "the believer's knowledge of God's will and purposes."[1] This particular meaning of "conscience" is derived from Romans 12.1–2, where Christians are called to worship God and not be conformed to this world, but rather to be "transformed by the renewal of your mind, that by testing you may discern what is the will of God, what is good and acceptable and perfect." It is for this reason that we are to submit ourselves to the governing authorities in such a way that we are not conformed to the world and God's revealed will is not compromised.[2] This is why Stephen Monsma said:

> As we Christian citizens vote, express our opinions, and in other ways act politically, it is essential for us to do so carefully and thoughtfully. An

1. Moo, 803.
2. Grimsrud, "Anabaptist Faith and American Democracy," 349.

> understanding of relevant biblical principles and of the factual situation will help us determine our priorities and ensure that we are supporting policy options that are indeed honoring to our Lord.[3]

Christians are to submit to the government of the United States of America by engaging the political process distinctly as Christians, utilizing both Scriptural and natural argumentation that presupposes our beliefs.

Christians are called "to give witness to all, including the state, by engaging and inviting all creation to realignment according to the way of God as demonstrated by Jesus."[4] We will be most effective within the socio-political realm by remaining true to our confession of faith.[5] This is why Monsma and Rogers said, "We are firmly convinced that God calls Christians to be active in the political world as Christians, that is, as persons whose stances and actions are shaped by their faith in Jesus Christ as the Lord of their lives and their Savior from sin."

To live out our faith actively within the public square flies in the face of "liberal theorists" like John Rawls, who believe "that Christians and other religious people should leave their faith convictions behind when they join the democratic conversation."[6] Not only do some say that

3. Monsma, 119.

4. Isaak, "The Christian Community and Political Responsibility," 40 and 44.

5. Grimsrud, 353.

6. Ibid., 353. Albert Mohler Jr. commented on the contemporary secularization of culture, saying, "That ideology, properly known as secularism, suggests that there is an *oughtness* to the secularization of the public space, that the culture *ought* to be established on purely secular terms without any reference at all to a theistic reality or a

Christians should leave their "faith convictions behind," but the late Richard Rorty believes that for Christians to live out their faith in the political realm is "dangerous to the health of democratic societies." He goes on to say, "religion is unobjectionable as long as it is privatized—as long as ecclesiastical intuitions do not attempt to rally the faithful behind political proposals and as long as believers and unbelievers agree to follow a policy of live and let live." [7] Such rhetoric exists beyond the comfort of a classroom and can readily be observed in our contemporary culture.

Though appealing on the surface, the contention for a strictly secular (non-theistic) state fails on several grounds.

First, secularism is as much of a religion as theistic religions, such as Christianity, Islam, and Judaism. Generally speaking, religion is understood as:

> A set of beliefs concerning the cause, nature, and purpose of the universe, esp. when considered as the creation of a superhuman agency or agencies, usually involving devotional and ritual observances, and often containing a moral code governing the conduct of human affairs; A specific fundamental set of beliefs and practices generally agreed upon by a number of persons or sects; The body of persons adhering to a particular set of beliefs and practices.[8]

Governments must deal with ultimate issues, such as life and death, and when governments address such issues they

---

theistic accountability" (Mohler Jr., *Culture Shift*, 8).

7. Rorty and Vattimo, *The Future of Religion*, 33.

8. "Religion," Dictionary.com, accessed October 17, 2010, http://dictionary.reference.com/browse/religion.

unavoidably cease to be secular.[9] As we previously saw, public policy and civil law is based upon some level of morality that implies what someone should and should not do. This is why "when states begin to affect laws and codify some morality, there is no way they can remain purely secular, because any question that addresses itself to the meaning of life and death . . . must be considered in terms much larger than secular theory will allow."[10] Besides, the very notion of secularism provides a level of moral "oughtness," in that governments ought to be secular.[11] This leads us to our second point.

Second, secularism is based upon ultimate beliefs as much as Christianity.[12] In the words of Nancy Pearcy, "no system of thought is a product purely of Reason—because Reason is not a repository of infallible, religiously autonomous truths, as Descartes and the other rationalists thought." She goes on to say, "Instead, it [reason] is simply a human capacity, the ability to reason from premises. The important question, then, is what a person accepts as ultimate premises, for they shape everything that follows."[13]

Just like an onion, if we were to peel back the layers of any set of ideas we would arrive at some starting point that serves as the very core, the very premise that undergirds

9. Mohler, 16.

10. Ibid., 16.

11. Ibid., 9.

12. Pearcy, 42.

13. Ibid., 41. Premise is defined as "a statement that is assumed to be true for the purpose of an argument from which a conclusion is drawn" ("Premise," Dictionary.com, accessed October 17, 2010, http://dictionary.reference.com/browse/premise.

their existence. "Every system of thought begins with some ultimate principle. If it does not begin with God, it will begin with some dimension of creation—the material, the spiritual, the biological, the empirical, or whatever."[14] It is for this reason that Pearcy contends, "In this sense, we could say that every alternative to Christianity is a religion. It may not involve ritual or worship services yet it identifies some principle or force in creation as the self-existent cause of everything else."[15] This is why I believe she is right when she concludes, "So the question is not which view is religious and which is purely rational; the question is which is true and which is false."[16] It seems, then, that the very notion of secularism is illusional.

Third, laws and public policy that revolve around mankind "as the measure of all things" cannot develop "standards of justice or values without God."[17] In other words, without an objective external moral standard, it would be impossible to settle disputes over justice and value. Besides, without an objective standard people can't accuse others of committing a crime, acts of unfairness, injustice, or even complain about the problem of evil and pain.[18] How can such accusations be made if morality is relegated to a personal opinion?

The unavoidable nature of moral absolutes in the public square is observed in the contention of secularists for

14. Ibid., 41.

15. Ibid., 41.

16. Ibid., 42.

17. McDowell, *A Ready Defense*, 317.

18. Beckwith and Koukl, 61–69; Geisler, *Baker Encyclopedia of Christian Apologetics*, 501–2.

the oughtness of a secular state. In the words of Norman Geisler, "'Ought' statements are moral statements, and 'ought never' statements are absolute moral statements. So, there is no way to avoid moral absolutes without affirming a moral absolute. Total moral relativism is self-defeating."[19]

Fourth, to exclude all non-secular discourse from law and public policy is a failure to distinguish between reason and content. In the words of Wayne Grudem:

> There were religious reasons behind many of our laws, but these laws do not "establish" a religion. All major religions have teachings against stealing, but laws against stealing do not "establish a religion."[20]

The same could be said for a litany of other issues today, such as the contention for the life of the unborn and the definition of marriage as between one man and one woman.

If secularist's arguments for the exclusion of non-secular religions from political discourse are successful, then votes cast in favor of legislation protecting the unborn or defining marriage as between one man and one woman could be invalidated on the grounds of their religious presuppositions.[21] This reality is evident in Judge Vaughn Walker's recent overturning of California's Proposition 8. Among the other influences on his decision, Judge Walker cited the "Religious beliefs that gay and lesbian relationships are sinful or inferior to heterosexual relationships

19. Geisler, 501.

20. Grudem, *Politics*, 31.

21. Ibid., 31.

harm gays and lesbians."[22] A similar decision has also been observed in the state of Colorado, where a constitutional amendment to define marriage between one man and one woman was overturned because the majority vote was based upon religious reasons.[23]

The exclusion of non-secular religious discourse from law and public policy also goes directly against the First Amendment's prohibition against inhibiting the free exercise of religion and freedom of speech.

Fifth, the notion that a strictly secular public square was intended by the First Amendment is not a historically tenable position. If the Founding Fathers' intent was to create an irreducibly secular government, then how do we reconcile the language of our country's founding documents and the very practices of the states and federal government during and after the drafting of the First Amendment? Consider just this small sampling:

> During the American Revolution, the Articles of War recommended that officers and men attend religious services with court-martials leveled against those who acted inappropriately.

22 Online: http://www.washingtontimes.com/news/2010/aug/11/proposition-8-judge-attacks-churches/. Al Mohler observed, "The religious liberty dimensions of the decision are momentous and deeply troubling. While Judge Walker declared that the religious freedoms of citizens and religious bodies were not violated because no such body is required to recognize or perform same-sex marriage, the very structure of his argument condemned religious and theological objections to homosexuality and same-sex marriage as both harmful and irrational" (Mohler, "Why the Proposition 8 Decision Matter," Christianity Today, accessed August 10, 2010, http://www.christianitytoday.com/ct/2010/augustweb-only/41.41.0.html.

23. Varnum v. Brien from Grudem, 32.

The signers of the Declaration of Independence agreed that the "Laws of Nature and of Nature's God" gave them the right to declare independence from Britain. What is more, they agreed that "governments are instituted among men" for the purpose of securing an individual's "unalienable Rights, that among these are Life, Liberty, and the pursuit of Happiness" that are endowed by their Creator. If a secular intent undergirded these documents, why then did the drafters and signers look to God as a means of validating the Declaration of Independence and the foundation to human liberty?[24]

One of the chief architects in drafting the First Amendment, James Madison, may have introduced legislation for disestablishing the Episcopal Church in Virginia (1785), but he also introduced legislation that same year to punish people who broke the Sabbath, provided for days of prayer and thanksgiving, and planned on backing religion with the force of law.[25]

After ratifying the First Amendment, the House of Representatives passed a resolution "calling for a day of national prayer and thanksgiving."[26]

State support of churches and religious requirements for political office continued well after the passage of the First Amendment.[27]

24. Ibid., 32.

25. Evans, *The Theme is Freedom*, 277–78.

26. Ibid., 285.

27 Ibid., 278.

> The Continental Congress appointed a Chaplain and opened the proceedings with prayer (1774); called for a public day of fasting and prayer and members attended an Anglican and Presbyterian service (1775); supported the printing of Bibles (1780); passed the Northwest Ordinance for various reasons, especially promoting "religion and morality"; and appropriated money for the Native Americans in Christian Education.[28]

If Thomas Jefferson adhered to modern day secularism, why did he frame "A Bill for Appointing Days of Public Fasting and Thanksgiving" in the late 1770s? And why, when Jefferson was Virginia's governor in 1779, did he assign a day "for publick and solemn thanksgiving and prayer to Almighty God?"[29] However, while serving as the President Jefferson refused to designate days for national fasting and thanksgiving. With conflicting decisions made, how then are we to reconcile his actions on the state and federal level? One possible reason for this discrepancy is that

28. Ibid., 278–81. Reasoning for this ordinance, John Quincy Adams said, "They were considered as savages, whom it was our policy and duty to use our influence in converting to Christianity and in ringing with the pale of civilization . . . We endeavored to bring them to the knowledge of religion and letters . . . We have had the rare good fortune of teaching them the arts of civilization and the doctrines of Christianity" (Evans, 280).

29. Daniel Dreisbach, "The Mythical 'Wall of Separation,'" Heritage Foundation, accessed December 15, 2010, http://www.heritage.org/research/reports/2006/06/the-mythical-wall-of-separation-how-a-misused-metaphor-changed-church-state-law-policy-and-discourse.

> the First Amendment "prohibited religious establishments by the federal government only."[30]

If a strict secular government was intended from the outset of our country, how can our country's history be reconciled with today's call for secularism? As M. Stanton Evans pointedly said, ". . . it can't."[31] The only way that we can reconcile a secularist notion with our country's history is to have it revised.

Thus, the call to submit to the government is the call to submit for the sake of conscience. And, as we just observed, this call is in no way a conflict of conscience with the government of the United States of America. At this point it is important to point out two different ways that our conscience will serve us as we do.

TWO WAYS THAT OUR CONSCIENCE SERVES US

Based on this passage (Rom 13.1–7), I believe there are two important ways that our conscience serves us:

1. Our conscience obligates us to be submissive to the governing authorities (Rom 13.1); and
2. Our conscience sets a limit on our submission to the governing authorities. For what is against our conscience cannot be done.[32]

Combining these two thoughts means that Christians are obligated to submit to the governing authorities and engage the political and social structures of our community

30. Ibid.
31. Evans, 281.
32. Stott, 342.

without giving up our allegiance to Jesus Christ. We do this not only because our conscience demands it, but for the sake of the Lord Jesus Christ Himself (1 Pet 2.13–15).

Our submission to the governing authorities of America as Christians is only impossible when political organizations rule out the redemptive force of Jesus Christ as a viable means by which they can achieve their goals for public policy and social betterment.[33] This doesn't mean that our positions and viewpoints must be accepted, but that we simply have the opportunity to live out our faith within the public square.

We are to submit ourselves to the governing authorities of the United States of America by influencing the Democratic process distinctly as Christians. We are told that submitting to every human institution is the will of God, and by doing so we are doing the right thing—unless, by submitting, we are doing what God forbids (or not doing what God commands). Our Christ-like submission to the government may very well "silence the ignorance of foolish men." We are to go out of our way and submit to the government right up to the point where obedience to the state would mean disobedience to God. There are many examples from Scripture and around the world that we could pull from, but let us just consider three: one from the Old Testament, one from the New Testament, and one from 2008.

In the second book of the Bible, Exodus, we read in the first chapter that the Egyptian Pharaoh ordered the Hebrew midwives to kill all baby boys as soon as they were born. But we are told that out of their fear of God they "did

33. Henry, 81.

not do as the king of Egypt had commanded them, but let the boys live." They feared God more than the government, and God honored their decision (Exod 1.8–19). In fact, for their obedience toward God, God honored these Hebrew midwives by establishing households for them (Exod 1.21).

In the fifth book of the New Testament, Acts, we are told of a time when Peter and the other apostles were brought before the Jewish government and forbidden to preach in the name of Jesus Christ. Acts 5.29 says that Peter and the apostles answered them, saying, "We must obey God rather than men."

The 2008 Summer Olympics were held in Beijing, China, where the government maintains a tight control over all religions. There are only two legal "Christian" churches in China, and they are both under the control of the Communist Party of China. It is illegal for Christians to have activities as groups in public places and in homes; it is illegal to have Sunday School; and the government, which controls the internet, blocks access to most Christian material online. If Chinese Christians, out of their obedience to God, are caught participating in any of these "illegal" acts, then the government will shut down their meeting and imprison everyone involved. This is another example of Christians breaking the law in order to obey God.

COMPROMISING IN THE PUBLIC SQUARE

It has been implied that faith and government are mutually exclusive. That is, you have to have one or the other. Phil Johnson, Executive Director of Grace to You, had the following to say:

> . . . in order to work in the realm of secular politics, you have to make certain compromises. Politics is built on compromise. Anybody who's involved in politics will affirm that for you. There are some things you cannot talk about in the political realm and the gospel is one of them. James Dobson's political allies in the realm of moral reform include multitudes who would not share his commitment to the gospel of the New Testament.[34]

Are we as Christians, then, supposed to exclude ourselves from the political arena since certain "compromises" are to be made? Are Christians inhibited from ever speaking about the Gospel publicly? Is there something wrong in working with non-Christians towards a common goal for the betterment of the community? Let's briefly explore these issues

I'm not sure what definition of compromise that Mr. Johnson was using in his above statement; however, the generally accepted definition of "compromise" is to settle a dispute by accepting "less than originally wanted."[35] Compromising, then, in the political process does not necessarily involve a compromise of one's convictions when working with others. It's entirely possible to compromise on tactics or policies without having to sell one's soul to the Devil.

34. Phil Johnson, "The Foolishness of Preaching the Gospel," Bible Bulletin Board, accessed December 15, 2010, http://www.biblebb.com/files/dobson.htm.

35. "Compromise," Encarta, accessed December 16, 2010, http://encarta.msn.com/dictionary_/compromise.html.

Stephen Monsma and Mark Rodgers label such compromises "half-a-loaf." That is, "someone who is working for a certain goal is willing to compromise and accept the partial achievement of that goal on the basis that half a loaf is better than none, as it is often put."

For example, "Practical policy making is a craft, and it is more often the art of the possible. Trade-offs are common. Should the minimum wage be increased to $10/hour, thereby providing a 'living wage' for low-income workers, or will a more modest increase ensure that fewer employees are laid off because they are no longer affordable to business?" Another example of successful political compromise is found in the process by which slavery was abolished in Britain.

From 1780–1807, politician and philanthropist William Wilberforce labored for the abolition of slavery in Britain. Wilberforce not only worked with non-Christians (Wilberforce himself wasn't converted to Christianity until 1786),[36] but he also had to settle for incremental policy changes instead of the complete abolition of slavery many times.[37] Since such compromises were made, are we to conclude that Wilberforce and company were wrong in accepting political compromises? I don't think so. These compromises accepted by Wilberforce were steps toward his ultimate goal.

Besides, as alluded to by Mr. Johnson, if it is wrong to work with non-Christians in the area of moral reform, then

36. Belmonte, *William Wilberforce*, 107.

37. For a thorough analysis of William Wilberforce's work in the abolition of slavery, see Belmonte, 96–151.

are we to conclude that William Wilberforce was wrong for having done so? Again, I don't think so.

As Christians we are more than capable of compromising in tactics and policies without having to compromise our faith in Jesus Christ. To work with non-Christians in political matters doesn't mean that we have to agree with them in their beliefs, just their political position.

LIVING FAITHFULLY IN THE PUBLIC SQUARE

Above, Mr. Johnson said, "There are some things you cannot talk about in the political realm and the gospel is one of them." Apparently Mr. Johnson believes that Christians cannot live out their faith in politics. I wonder if this goes only for government, or if this includes all areas of society?

Living as a Christian in the world will not make us popular. If anything, we're promised the opposite in John 15.19; 17.14. A cursory look at music, movies, and television is enough to know that the messages of these media are generally at odds with the message of Christianity, which is enough to say that living as a Christian isn't the latest fad. This, combined with the trajectory of public policies' secular influence still doesn't mean that we are to compartmentalize our faith in the public square. Though it would be challenging and difficult to live unabashedly as a Christian while serving in politics, this doesn't mean that it has not or cannot be done. Again, let's consider William Wilberforce as an example.

I imagine the political environment inhabited by William Wilberforce in the 18th and 19th centuries was no less welcoming of Christians as our contemporary democratic process is. Regardless of the similarities in our political environments, Wilberforce lived unashamedly as a Christian. In 1797 he penned what is known today as *Real Christianity*, a stinging indictment against what he called "cultural Christians." He wrote this piece as a means of arousing people to faith in Jesus Christ. In his own words from the introduction, Wilberforce said:

> I would suggest that faith is everyone's business. The advance or decline of faith is so intimately connected to the welfare of a society that it should be of particular interest to a politician.[38]

You can read the rest of the book for yourself, but I will let you know that Wilberforce unhesitatingly lived and spoke his faith in Jesus Christ in both word and deed. This was not done exclusively in the privacy of his own home or on Sunday mornings, but rather publicly, often to the indifference of many. What Wilberforce exemplified is that it is possible to serve Christ faithfully and wholeheartedly in public affairs without compromising his or her convictions.

38. Wilberforce, *Real Christianity*, 17.

7

A Call to Action

It is my belief that what has been presented thus far is a Biblical case for Christians to influence the democratic process in America. In fulfilling this call upon our lives, let us not hesitate to unabashedly live out our faith in Jesus Christ as we submit to the government in a limited way for the sake of wrath, conscience, and our LORD. May we proceed with the love that characterizes followers of Christ, so that our participation does not undermine our witness.

Our submission to and engagement with the government of the United States of America is much more than tolerating it as a necessary evil. As Christians we must submit to the governing authorities of America by honoring its representatives, paying taxes, promoting justice and the welfare of all, and praying for those who serve within it, regardless of their political persuasion.[1]

Finally, aside from running for political office, the primary way to be involved and make a difference is by voting and holding our representatives accountable. It is our responsibility to be informed voters who look upon the

1. Stott, 347.

candidates and their parties or affiliations through a distinct Christian worldview.

CLOSING PRAYER

"Now may the God of peace who brought again from the dead our Lord Jesus, the great shepherd of the sheep, by the blood of the eternal covenant, equip you with everything good that you may do his will, working in us that which is pleasing in his sight, through Jesus Christ, to whom be glory forever and ever. Amen."

Bibliography

Barton, David. *Original Intent: The Courts, the Constitution, and Religion*. Aledo: WallBuilder Press, 2000.

Bauer, Walter. *A Greek English Lexicon of the New Testament and Other Early Christian Literature*, 2d. Edited by Arndt, William, Gingrich, Wilbur, and Frederick W. Danker. Chicago: University of Chicago Press, 1979.

Beckwith, Francis, and Gregory Koukl. *Relativism: Feet Firmly Planted in Mid-Air*. Grand Rapids: Baker Books, 1998.

Before the Human Rights Commission of the State of New Mexico. "Vanessa Willock v. Elane Photography LLC." Accessed December 10, 2010. http://media.npr.org/documents/2008/jun/photography.pdf.

Belmonte, Kevin Belmonte. *William Wilberforce: A Hero for Humanity*. Grand Rapids: Zondervan, 2007.

Bennett, John C. *Christians and the State*. New York: Charles Scribner's Sons, 1958.

Calvin, John. *Commentaries on the Epistle of Paul the Apostle to the Romans*. Translated by John Owen. *Christian Classics Ethereal Library*. Accessed December 5, 2010. http://www.ccel.org/ccel/calvin/calcom38.xvii.ii.html.

Colson, Charles W. *Kingdoms in Conflict: An Insider's Challenging View of Politics, Power, and the Pulpit*. Grand Rapids: William Morrow and Zondervan Publishing House, 1987.

DeWeese, Garrett, and J.P. Moreland. *Philosophy Made Slightly Less Difficult: A Beginners Guide to Life's big Questions*. Downers Grove: InterVarsity Press, 2005.

Dictionary. "Religion." Accessed October 17, 2010. http://dictionary.reference.com/browse/religion.

———. "Premise." Accessed October 17, 2010. http://dictionary.reference.com/browse/premise.

Dreisbach, Daniel. The Mythical "Wall of Separation": How a Misused Metaphor Changed Church-State Law, Policy, and Discourse." *The Heritage Foundation,* June 23, 2006. Accessed December 15, 2010. http://www.heritage.org/research/reports/2006/06/the-mythical-wall-of-separation-how-a-misused-metaphor-changed-church-state-law-policy-and-discourse.

Eidsmoe, John. *Christianity and the Constitution: The Faith of Our Founding Fathers.* Grand Rapids: Baker Books, 1987.

Encarta. "Compromise." Accessed December 16, 2010. http://encarta.msn.com/dictionary_/compromise.html.

Evans, M. Stanton. *The Theme is Freedom: Religion, Politics, and the America Tradition.* Washington, D.C.: Regnery Publishing, Inc., 1994.

FindLaw. "Boy Scouts of America et. al., v. Dale." Accessed May 19, 2011. http://caselaw.lp.findlaw.com/scripts/getcase.pl?court=US&vol=000&invol=99-699.

FOXNews.com. "Phoenix Pastor Draws Protests After Telling Church He Prays for Obama's Death." *Fox News*, August 31, 2009. Accessed December 10, 2010. http://www.foxnews.com/politics/2009/08/31/phoenix-pastor-draws-protests-telling-church-prays-obamas-death/.

France, R.T. "The Gospel of Matthew." In *New International Commentary on the New Testament,* edited by Ned B. Stonehouse. F.F. Bruce, and Gordon D. Fee Grand Rapids: William B. Eerdmans Publishing Co., 2007.

Gallagher, Maggie. "Banned in Boston: The Coming Conflict Between Same-Sex Marriage and Religious Liberty." *The Weekly Standard*, May 15, 2006. Accessed December 10, 2010. http://www.weeklystandard.com/Content/Public/Articles/000/000/012/191kgwgh.asp.

———. *The Case for Marriage: Why Married People are Happier, Healthier, and Better off Financially.* New York: Broadway Books, 2000.

Geisler, Norman L. *Baker Encyclopedia of Christian Apologetics.* Grand Rapids: Baker Books, 1999.

Greenberg, Edward S., and Benjamin I. Page. *The Struggle for Democracy.* 6th ed. New York: Longman, 2003.

Grimsrud, Ted. "Anabaptist Faith and American Democracy." *The Mennonite 7.19* (2004): 14–15. Accessed December 10, 2011. http://www.themennonite.org/attachments/pdfs/0000/0071/Issue19-7.pdf.

Grudem, Wayne. *Politics According to the Bible.* Grand Rapids: Zondervan, 2010.

Gundry, Robert H. *A Survey of the New Testament.* Grand Rapids: Zondervan, 2003.

Hart, Darryl. *A Secular Faith: Why Christianity Favors the Separation of Church and State.* Chicago: Ivan R. Dee, 2006.

Henry, Carl F.H. *The Uneasy Conscience of Modern Fundamentalism.* Grand Rapids: William B. Eerdmans Publishing Co., 1947.

Hoekema, Anthony A. "Amillennialism." Accessed December 10, 2010. http://www.the-highway.com/amilc_Hoekema.html.

Institute for American Values. "Can Government Strengthen Marriage? Evidence from the Social Science." Accessed December 5, 2010. http://www.marriagedebate.com/pdf/Can%20Government%20Strengthen%20Marriage.pdf.

Isaak Jon. "The Christian Community and Political Responsibility: Romans 13:1–7." *Direction 32.1* (2203): 32–46. Accessed December 10, 2011. http://www.directionjournal.org/article/?1287.

Jeffers, James S. *The Greco-Roman World of the New Testament: Exploring the Background of Early Christianity.* Downers Grove: InterVarsity Press, 1999.

Johnson, Phil. "The Foolishness of Preaching the Gospel." *Bible Bulletin Board.* Accessed December 15, 2010. http://www.biblebb.com/files/dobson.htm.

Kittel, Gerhard, and Gerhard Friedrich. *Theological Dictionary of the New Testament: Abridged in One Volume.* Translated by Geoffrey Bromiley. Grand Rapids: William B. Eerdmans Publishing Co., 1985.

Kinnaman, David, and Gabe Lyons. U*nChristian: What a New Generation Really Thinks About Christianity . . . and Why it Matters.* Grand Rapids: BakerBooks, 2007.

Kostenberger, Andreas J. *God Marriage, and Family: Rebuilding the Biblical Foundations.* Wheaton: Crossway Books, 2004.

Kyle, Richard. "Anabaptist and Reformed Attitudes Towards Civil Government: A Factor in Political Involvement." *Direction 14.1* (1985). Accessed December 10, 2010, http://www.directionjournal.org/article/?514.

MacArthur, John. *Why Government Can't Save You: An Alternative to Political Activism*. Nashville: Word Publishing, 2000.

———. "Daniel: God's Control over Rulers and Nations." In *MacArthur Bible Studies*. Nashville: W. Publishing Group, 2000.

Macedo, Diane. "Praying Outside Clinic Gets Man Disorderly Conduct Charge." *Fox News*, August 2, 2010. Accessed December 10, 2010. http://www.foxnews.com/us/2010/07/31/pub-chicago-man-charged-disorderly-conduct-praying-outside-planned-parenthood/.

McDowell, Josh. *A Ready Defense*. Nashville: Thomas Nelson, 1992.

Miller, Joshua Rhett. "Lawsuit Claims College Ordered Student to Alter Religious Views on Homosexuality, or Be Dismissed." *Fox News*, July 27, 2010. Accessed December 10, 2010. http://www.foxnews.com/us/2010/07/27/georgia-university-tells-student-lose-religion-lawsuit-laims/?test=faces.

Minnery, Tom. *Why You Can't Stat Silent: A Biblical Mandate to Shape our Culture*. Wheaton: Tyndale House Publishers, Inc., 2001.

Mohler Jr., R. Albert. *Culture Shift: Engaging Current Issues With Timeless Truth*. Colorado Springs: Multnomah Books, 2008.

———. "Why the Proposition 8 Decision Matter." *ChristianityToday*, August 5, 2010. Accessed August 10, 2010. http://www.christianitytoday.com/ct/2010/augustweb-only/41.41.0.html.

Monsma, Steve. *Healing for a Broken World: Christian Perspectives on Public Policy*. Wheaton: Crossway Books, 2008.

Monsma, Stephen, and Mark Rogers. "In the Arena." In *Toward an Evangelical Public Policy: Political Strategies for the Health of the Nation*, eds. Ronald J. Sider and Diane Knippers. Grand Rapids: Baker Books, 2005.

Moo, Douglas J. "The Epistle to the Romans." In *The New International Commentary on the New Testament*, edited by Ned B. Stonehouse. F.F. Bruce, and Gordon D. Fee. Grand Rapids: William B. Eerdmans Publishing Company, 1996.

Morris, Leon. "The Epistle to the Romans." In *The Pillar New Testament Commentary*, edited by D.A. Carson. Grand Rapids: William B. Eerdmans Publishing Co., 1988.

Mott, Stephen Charles.*Biblical Ethics and Social Change*. New York: Oxford University Press, 1982.

Mounce, William D. *Basics of Biblical Greek*. Grand Rapids: Zondervan, 2003.

———. *The Analytical Lexicon to the Greek New Testament*. Grand Rapids: Zondervan Publishing House, 1993.

Neufeld, Matthew G. "Submission to Governing Authorities: A Study of Romans 13.1–7." *Biblical Interpretation* 23.2 (1994): 90–97.

Noebel, David A. *Understanding the Times: The Religious Worldviews of Our Day and the Search for Truth*. Colorado: Association of Christian Schools International, 1995.

Osborne, Grant R. T*he Hermeneutical Spiral: A Comprehensive Introduction to Biblical Interpretation*. Downers Grove: InterVarsity Press, 1991.

Pearcy, Nancy. *Total Truth: Liberating Christianity from its Cultural Captivity*. Wheaton: Crossway Books, 2004.

Pendleton, David A. "The Government Should Legislate Morality." I) n *American Values: Opposing Viewpoints*, ed. Jennifer A. Hurley. San Diego: Greenhaven Press Inc., 2000.

Piper, John. *What Jesus Demands from the World*. Wheaton: Crossway Books, 2006.

Rorty, Richard Rorty and Gianni Vattimo, *The Future of Religion* (Columbia University Press, 2005), 33.

Smidt, Corwin. "The Principled Pluralist Perspective." In *Church, State and Public Justice: Five Views*, ed. P.C. Kemeny. Downers Grove: InterVarsity Press, 2007.

Sproul, R.C. *Essential Truths of the Christian Faith: 100 Key Teachings in Plain Language*. Carol Stream: Tyndale House Publishers, Inc., 1992.

———. "The Threefold Use of the Law." *Monergism*. Accessed December 15, 2010. http://www.monergism.com/thethreshold/articles/onsite/sproul/threefold_law.html.

Starnes, Todd. "Court Upholds Expulsion of Counseling Student Who Opposes Homosexuality." *Fox News*, July 28, 2010. Accessed

December 10, 2010. http://www.foxnews.com/us/2010/07/28/court-university-expel-student-opposes-homosexuality/.

Stott, John R. "The Message of Romans." In *The Bible Speaks Today,* edited by J.A. Mortyer, John R. W. Stott, and Derek Tidball Downers Grove: Inter-Varsity Press, 1994.

Supreme Court of the United States. "Christian Legal Society Chapter of the University of California, Hastings College of the Law, AKA Hastings Christian Fellowship v. Martinez et al." Accessed May 19, 2011. http://www.supremecourt.gov/opinions/09pdf/08-1371.pdf.

The Center for Public Justice. "Guidelines for Government and Citizenship: Government." Accessed December, 10, 2010. http://www.cpjustice.org/content/government.

The Lausanne Movement. "The Lausanne Covenant: Christian Social Responsibility." Accessed May 19, 2011. http://www.lausanne.org/covenant.

Turner, David L. "Matthew." In *Baker Exegetical Commentary on the New Testament,* edited by Robert W. Yarbrough and Robert H. Stein. Grand Rapids: Baker Academic, 2008.

United States District Court: District of Massachusetts. "David Parker, et al., Plaintiffs, v. William Hurley, et al., Defendants." Accessed May 19, 2011. http://www.massresistance.org/docs/parker_lawsuit/motion_to_dismiss_2007/order_motion_to_dismiss_022307.pdf.

Van Til, Henry R. *The Calvinistic Concept of Culture.* Grand Rapids: Baker Academic, 1959.

VanDrunen, David. "Bearing Sword in the State, Turning Cheek in the Church: A Reformed Two-Kingdoms Interpretation of Matthew 5:38–42." *Themelios* 34.3 (2009): 322–334. Accessed December 5, 2010. http://www.thegospelcoalition.org/publications/34-3/bearing-sword-in-the-state-turning-cheek-in-the-church.

Warner, Greg. "Call to Kill Terrorists 'In the Name of the Lord' Sparks Outcry." *The Baptist Standard,* November 11, 2004. Accessed October 1, 2008. http://www.baptiststandard.com/index.php?option=com_content&task=view&id=2704&Itemid=12.

Westboro Baptist Church. Accessed December 10, 2010. http://www.godhatesfags.com/.

Wikipedia. "One-Child Policy." Last modified May 11, 2011. http://en.wikipedia.org/wiki/One-child_policy#Human_rights.

Wilberforce, William. *Real Christianity*, ed. Bob Beltz..Ventura: Regal Books, 2006.

Williamson, G.I. *The Westminster Confession of Faith: For Study* Classes. Phillipsburg: P & R Publishing, 2004.

Wisdom, Alan F.H. "Wisdom: Marriage over the rainbow: Ruling would make traditional believers enemies of the state." *The Washington Times*, August 11, 2010. Accessed December 10, 2010. http://www.washingtontimes.com/news/2010/aug/11/proposition-8-judge-attacks-churches/.

Wolters, Albert M. *Creation Regained: Biblical Basics for a Reformational Worldview*. Grand Rapids: William B. Eerdmans Publishing Co., 1985.

Wright, Joseph. "Reducing Abortion in America: Beyond *Roe v. Wade*." *Catholics United*, August, 2008. Accessed December 10, 2010. http://www.nd.edu/~cdems/College_Democrats_of_Notre_Dame/College_Democrats_of_Notre_Dame/Issues_files/reducing-abortion-in-america.pdf.

Yoder, John Howard. *The Politics of Jesus*. Grand Rapids: William B. Eerdmans Publishing Company, 1994.

www.ingramcontent.com/pod-product-compliance
Lightning Source LLC
Chambersburg PA
CBHW071100090426
42737CB00013B/2402

9781610976077